Reflecting upon some problems of the moral life, Gilbert Meilaender considers their difficulties within a vision that accentuates not only the limits, but also the promise, of the Christian story. Created by God as finite beings, we make particular attachments. Redeemed by God for a community transcending nature and history, our love always carries us beyond the special bonds of time and place. We live, therefore, with a sense of permanent tension.

If this tension heightens our sense of the perplexities of life, it should not free us from the obligation to probe, clarify, and (where we can) resolve some of those difficulties. The author holds that theological ethics must clarify the direction for growth and development within the Christian life. He undertakes such analysis, emphasizing throughout the limits of the human condition, the importance of our nature as embodied persons, and the danger and pretension in some of our attempts to take control of and master human life. This Christian vision is developed in chapters that explore a range of moral problems, such as abortion, artificial reproduction, euthanasia, care for defective infants, provision of artificial nutrition and hydration, and marital and political community. These are throughout, however, *theological* explorations. Taken together they illumine not only particular problems of the moral life but a vision of life — classically Christian in its conception, humane in its care for particular bonds of attachment, and modest in its recognition of moral limits on our ability to seek the good.

Meilaender has developed a broad recognition both among scholars and students of ethics and among interested general readers. He has the capacity to throw fresh angles of vision on complex problems so as to help both the sophisticated and the uninitiated reader to think more penetratingly about moral questions.

The Limits of Love:
Some Theological Explorations

Also by Gilbert Meilaender

The Taste for the Other: The Social and Ethical Thought of C. S. Lewis
Friendship: A Study in Theological Ethics
The Theory and Practice of Virtue

The Limits of Love
Some Theological Explorations

Gilbert Meilaender

The Pennsylvania State University Press
University Park and London

Grateful acknowledgment is made to the editors and publishers for permission to reprint portions of this book that have been published previously.
"Goodbye, Sally, Goodbye" was first published in *The Cresset* 48 (November 1984): 18–19.
"Theology in Stories" was first published in *Word & World* 1 (Summer 1981): 222–29.
"The Place of Ethics in the Theological Task" draws upon material first published in two places: "The Place of Ethics in the Theological Task," in *Currents in Theology and Mission* 4 (August 1979): 196–203; and "Living with Aristotle and Luther," in *Forum Letter* 14 (March 1, 1985): 7f.
An earlier version of "The Fetus as Parasite and Mushroom" appeared in *Linacre Quarterly* 46 (May 1979): 126–35. 850 Elm Grove Rd., Elm Grove, WI 53122. Subscription rate: $20 per year; $5 per single issue.
"Against Abortion," now considerably reworked, appeared in *Linacre Quarterly* 45 (May 1978): 165–78.
"Euthanasia and Christian Vision" is reprinted by permission of the publisher from *Thought* 57 (December 1982): 465–75. New York: Fordham University Press, 1982. Copyright © 1982 by Fordham University Press.
"If This Baby Could Choose . . . ," now somewhat reworked, was originally published in *Linacre Quarterly* 49 (November 1982): 313–21.
"Withdrawing Food and Water" was originally published under the title "On Removing Food and Water: Against the Stream," in *Hastings Center Report* 14 (December 1984): 11–13.
An earlier version of "Marital Community" was published under the title "Embodiment: Taking It Seriously," in *Concordia Journal* 5 (November 1979): 216–21.
"Political Community" was first published under the title "Individuals in Community: An Augustinian Vision," in *The Cresset* 47 (November 1983): 5–10.

Library of Congress Cataloging-in-Publication Data

Meilaender, Gilbert, 1946–
    The limits of love.

    Bibliography: p.
    Includes index.
    1. Christian ethics. 2. Sexual ethics.
3. Medical ethics. 4. Social ethics. I. Title.
BJ1251.M49 1987   241   87-42548
ISBN 0-271-00611-0

To Ellen,
who has often been my conscience

Contents

Foreword

This is a book about moral problems—but about how those problems look from a particular religious perspective. It is, therefore, at least as much a book about understanding our human nature within the contours of the story the Bible tells. My focus is on the *limits* of love—limits to what we can accomplish, limits to what we should do in a good cause, limits to our attempts to be more than finite creatures. Much of the pang and pathos of the Christian vision, and many of the greatest temptations for faith, arise from the need to make the best of the moral limits our nature places upon us. We are made for God and therefore are not simply finite beings—but we are not to try to be gods. The tensions created by that duality in our nature are the stuff of much that is most troubling in the moral life.

The second chapter, "Theology in Stories," uses the writings of C. S. Lewis to explore this understanding of what it means to be human. This sets the stage for my attempts in later chapters to affirm the finite attachments within which we live, while acknowledging the limits that ought to govern our attempts to deal with the pain and anguish these attachments often bring. Human life cannot be understood properly if it is isolated from the God-relation in which, whether we know it or not, we live and move and have our being. When we think about human communities, or about individual lives in their beginning and ending, we are thinking about human beings who exist as creatures of God and are made for communion in love with God. One might, of course, conclude from this that reflection on moral problems is of little importance and that, instead, we should simply seek the virtue that is love for God. Chapter 3 develops and considers this theological challenge to the very enterprise of ethics. I do not deny the force of this challenge, but I do try to offer reasons for probing as deeply as we are able the shape of the moral life, the freedom love brings, and the limits love should acknowledge.

The chapters in Parts 2 and 3 do some of that probing. They take up a variety of disputed issues that surround life's beginning and ending. About each problem there is more to be said, and there are always more problems to be explored. But I offer here analysis and reflection that consider the limits of the human condition, the moral significance of our nature as embodied persons, the dangers of a love that knows no limit, and the impact of Christian vision upon the moral life. These are, throughout, theological explorations. Taken together they are intended to illumine not only some difficult problems but also a vision of life—one that is, I think and hope, Christian in its conception and structure. The two chapters in Part 4 are different in that they do not focus on particular problems, but the basic themes remain very much the same. The chapter on marital community applies a perspective that emphasizes the moral significance of our finite, embodied nature to one of the most fundamental human bonds. And the last chapter, on political community, seeks to develop one of the permanent limits with which the moral life must come to terms. If we—finite and limited creatures that we are—are made for God, we must resist the temptation to imagine that any community in our pilgrim history could be more than a station on the way. This is, quite often, a political temptation, but it should be resisted on theological grounds.

Finally, a word may be in order about the first chapter. One referee of an earlier manuscript of this book—a version in which this chapter appeared at a different point—commented that the chapter, though valuable, was "out of sync" with the rest of the book. And that was not a comment about the chapter's placement! I cannot deny the correctness of that reader's perception, for the first chapter *is* different from anything that follows. But not, I think, unrelated, for in it the central themes and vision of the book find expression. My solution to the reader's friendly criticism has, therefore, been to place this chapter first— recognizing both the sense in which it differs from anything that follows *and* the sense in which it introduces what follows. More generally, I want to thank Philip Winsor, senior editor at The Pennsylvania State University Press, for finding two readers whose able and perceptive comments helped me to understand more clearly what this book is about. I am pleased to have found in their comments and suggestions another of those finite attachments through which human life is sustained and enriched.

Part One
Ethics and Theology

1

Goodbye, Sally, Goodbye

Four days old, she came to us. How tiny is a newborn in the crib! Eight months old, she left us—going to her adoptive parents. How much living is packed into thirty-two weeks.

She has what we wanted for her, what every foster child needs: a good home, loving parents. Why, then, should it hurt? Partly, no doubt, because we desire for her—as for anyone we love—not only what is good, but the good *we* can give. Those who—waxing philosophical or, worse, abstractly theological—think this bad or call it selfish have much to learn about what it means to be human. Not to treasure the good that *we* can give would mean to love no one in particular, to let the heart be tied to no time, place, or person. As if the neighbor who is to be loved in God were not always a particular person.

Yet, it would be wrong to want the good we can give more than the good she truly needs. Wrong because it would stunt her and would not permit the good to flourish fully in her life. And so a gracious God goes to work on us to broaden and deepen our love—to help us love more than the limited good that we alone bestow. And it hurts. Which means, contrary to what we often say, that grace hurts.

I first learned this truth from C. S. Lewis, who drives it home most powerfully in *A Grief Observed,* a book written out of a deep sense of loss. For example:

If a mother is mourning not for what she has lost but for what her dead child has lost, it is a comfort to believe that the child has not lost the end for which it was created. . . . A comfort to the God-aimed eternal spirit within her. But not to her motherhood. The specifically maternal happiness must be written off. Never, in any place or time, will she have her son on her knees, or bathe him, or tell him a story, or plan for his future, or see her grandchild.

And in her own way, Sally has reinforced the lesson learned from Lewis: that it is painful to learn to love the good *wherever* it is given and by *whomever* it is bestowed.

How much she taught for one so little! How clear she made the importance of eschatology—the sense of an ending—in the Christian life. She came to us at a very busy time, when I was already burdened with too much work. Even so, I noticed how careful I was not to ignore her, to pay attention to her no matter how busy I might be. Far more careful, I am afraid, than I have sometimes been with my own children. Not fair to them? Perhaps. But I know why. They—their future joined with mine—can all too easily be taken for granted, as if stories never ended. She came with a day's notice and would leave with little more, as if in the middle of a chapter. We always knew that, and so each day had to be savored, for we lived constantly with the sense of an ending near at hand.

Such a little teacher, but she made it clear that all our days and hours are equidistant from eternity; none is merely preparation for some future that may never come. Too often we live our lives and organize those of our children as if days, weeks, even years were only preparation for something that lies ahead. We study in high school—so we can attend the college of our choice. We study in college—the better to land a good job. We work—in order to vacation. We wait for the days when we won't be so busy or when we'll have more money. We live in the future—forgetting that, unlike the present, it may never come. Remember the lilies of the field; they neither toil nor spin. Eight months can be a life. Often is. Our world thinks mainly in terms of potential and achievement. But Sally's academic and vocational "achievements" will be for others to enjoy. For us it was enough just to applaud when she stood in her crib, to laugh when she smiled.

From Kierkegaard, I think, I learned about the selflessness of true love. We love another best, he says, when it would be true to say, "He stands alone—by my help." And then, commenting on the significance of the dash in that sentence, he adds:

> In this little sentence the infinity of thought is contained in the most profound way, the greatest contradiction overcome. He stands alone—this is the highest; he stands alone—nothing else do you see. You see no aid or assistance, no awkward bungler's hand holding on to him any more than it occurs to the person himself that someone has helped him. No, he stands alone—by another's help. But this help is hidden, . . . it is hidden behind a dash.

And in her own way, Sally has driven home the lesson that love must not snatch. Embarrassing but true that we should learn the lesson more vividly from her than we sometimes do from the story of one who, though in the form of God, did not count equality with God a thing to be snatched. But it is true that love cannot always seek to possess. Sally's leaving brought pain in part because we would not want her, even for a few days, to feel that we whom she trusted had abandoned her.

And yet, in all our loves we must learn that there are limits to the care we can give. When we bring our children to baptism, we hand them over into the keeping of another. When we intercede in prayer for them, we admit that we cannot really care for them, and, once again, we give up our hold on them. Still, we may go for years without being asked—really being asked in a way we cannot ignore—to hand them over. We may deceive ourselves into thinking that we are sufficient caretakers for them. But Sally is a cure for such deceptions, and she has taught the lesson all too well in her leaving.

Ah, Sally, you have taught some profound theological truths to one not entirely ignorant of theology—to all of us. You have transformed a twelve-year-old boy who didn't want to be bothered by the presence of a baby into one who would take you from your crib and play with you early in the morning while others slept. You have satisfied the need of a nine-year-old girl to be maternal—and the need of a six-year-old to love the younger sibling she never had. Your sheer delight at waking reminded us all that joy really does come in the morning, that the new day is a gift—a lesson somehow forgotten as we grow older. You were, without any of our adult self-consciousness, eager to receive love, and have given as freely as you received.

All love truly given and received is taken up into the life of God who *is* and who is love. Hence, love abides, and though we often say goodbye, our loves are completed in the fullness of that divine life. Consider the relation "lover-beloved"—united by the hyphen that is love. Since love abides, Kierkegaard was right to say that the lover keeps the hyphen. And if separation comes and there remains only "lover-"? What then? Then the hyphenated word is not yet complete! Then we are to think not of a sentence fragment but of an unfinished sentence.

So let me memorialize a great teacher of theology. Those short legs, that deep voice so lovely in its cooing when she called. That mouth wide open in her noiseless laugh of delight (and wide open to get more of that first popsicle). That almost preternatural ability to behave quietly in public. The smile that came suddenly, coaxing one from us in return. That knowing look as she went once again for the television cord. And on that day so like life because such a blend of joy and sadness, the tiny red-haired girl, lovely in her green dress and in the patent-leather shoes (her first) that kept her from chewing on her toes.

We shall not let go the hyphen. Goodbye, Sally, goodbye.

2

Theology in Stories

In one of C. S. Lewis's stories, *The Voyage of the Dawn Treader,*[1] Lucy, Edmund, and Eustace have been whisked magically off into Narnia and are now sailing with King Caspian and his crew on a quest. Caspian is seeking some lost lords of Narnia as well as the end of the world ("the utter East"). They have many adventures—some merely strange, others dangerous. The adventure that concerns us comes when they arrive at the island of the Dufflepuds. These strange creatures (who have one large foot on which they hop about and who are not particularly intelligent) have, for reasons we need not concern ourselves with, been made invisible. In order to become visible again they need a young girl to go into the Magician's house, up to the second floor, and find the spell in the Magician's book that will make them visible once more. And they are determined not to permit Caspian's party to leave their island until Lucy consents to undertake this task.

Since it seems they have little choice—battling invisible antagonists is rather hard—Lucy agrees to brave the frightening house. She finds the book and begins turning pages looking for the spell. As she does so, however, she becomes engrossed in the various spells she finds there and reads large portions of the book. At one point she finds a spell "for the refreshment of the spirit" (p. 130). It turns out to be "more like a story than a spell." She begins to read, and "before she had read to the bottom of the page she had forgotten that she was reading at all. She was living in the story as if it were real . . ." (p. 130). When she finishes it, she feels that it is the loveliest story she has ever heard and wishes she could have gone on reading it for ten years.

She decides that she will, at least, read the story again but discovers that the pages will not turn backwards. " 'Oh what a shame!' said Lucy. 'I did so want to read it again. Well, at least I must remember it!' " (p. 130). But she finds, unfortunately, that she cannot really remember the plot of the story. It all begins to fade in her memory. "And she never could remember; and ever since that day what Lucy means by a good story is a story which reminds her of the forgotten story in the Magician's book" (p. 131).

Story as Refreshment and Frustration

We will not, I think, fully understand the wide appeal of Lewis's writings until we think carefully about the importance of stories for communicating Christian belief. Lewis often depicts the whole of life in terms of what we might call the Christian story of creation, fall, incarnation, redemption, and resurrection.[2] Beyond that, however, Lewis has, I believe, a strong sense of what Stephen Crites has called "the narrative quality of experience."[3] The very nature of human existence—conceived in Christian terms—is best understood within narrative.

Anyone who has read very far in Lewis will have encountered his characteristic theme of "romantic longing," or *Sehnsucht*. It is, in many ways, Lewis's restatement of the Augustinian theme of the restless heart. We are, as Lewis says in "The Weight of Glory," always trying to capture something, trying "to get in."[4] We want to ride time, not be ridden by it, "to cure that always aching wound . . . which mere succession and mutability inflict upon us."[5] The human being is, we may say, both finite and free: a bodily creature living in space and time, yet desiring to transcend such finite limitations and rest in God. The crucial question, of course, is whether such a creature is an absurdity or whether this desired fulfillment is attainable. If fulfillment of the longing that is integral to our being is impossible, then we really are absurd creatures—and it would be better simply to acknowledge the search as futile and endless, to vow with Faust never to say to any moment, "Stay a while, you are so lovely." Lewis is concerned with this question, concerned to know whether finite creatures such as we are can find any spell that offers genuine "refreshment of the spirit"—lasting refreshment of which we cannot be deprived by the corrosive powers of time.

The spell, if there is one, is not available in abstract, theoretical reasoning. Built into our thinking is a kind of frustration: A gap always exists between experiencing a thing and thinking about that thing. In thinking "about" anything we abstract ourselves from it, begin to separate it into its parts, and lose it as an object of contemplation. That is, while thinking about it we are cut off from experiencing it. A man cannot—the example is Lewis's—experience loving a woman if he is busy thinking about his technique.[6]

Lewis searches, therefore, for some other way—some means other than abstract thought to find the "refreshment of the spirit" for which human beings seem to be made. One way to such refreshment, a way that always attracted Lewis, lies in myth. On his somewhat stipulative definition, myth is extraliterary.[7] The fact that it must be communicated in words is almost accidental, for it is not so much a narration as it is a permanent object of contemplation—more like a thing than a story. That is to say, in myth we experience something timeless. Experiencing a myth is more like tasting than thinking, concrete rather than abstract. Yet it is also very different from other tastings, for it seems to bring experience not of some isolated tidbit of life that passes away but of what has timeless, universal significance.

We can, of course, also think "about" the universal and in that way move beyond isolated particulars of life. But this gives no *experience* of what is timeless, no experience of anything that may satisfy the longing of the human spirit to transcend the constraints of our finite condition. Instead, thinking about what is universal and timeless—which simultaneously cuts us off from experiencing it—is merely one more testimony to thought's built-in frustration. Myth provides, if only for a moment, what we desire: to break through to some great truth in which the heart can rest and which can give coherence to the isolated particulars of life. It offers what no other experience can: an actual tasting of a reality that transcends our finite existence. It brings us briefly into a world more real than our own, so real that any talk "about" it would have to be metaphorical.

However, myth offers no permanent peace for the quarrel between the two sides of our nature—our freedom and finitude. For a brief moment finitude is transcended, we are free of temporal constraints, and the transcendent is comfortingly passive. But the truth we are given in myth is not really a truth to live by in our here and now, for we live as creatures both free *and* finite. Because this is the case, Lewis looks elsewhere—away from myth to story—in order to find that "refreshment of the spirit" we desire. Although story cannot in any single moment of experience overcome the tension between finitude and freedom in the human being as completely as can myth, it points toward a more lasting peace—a peace we can live. Lewis discusses the genre of story in his essay "On Stories."[8] We can begin at the literary level and move toward the theological.

The story is, Lewis thinks, different from the novel. The novel concerns itself with delineation of character, criticism of social conditions, and so forth. Nor is the story merely, as some think, a vehicle of excitement and danger—anxious tension and, then, relief when the moment of danger passes. Lewis suggests that, at least for some readers, something more is going on when they read a story. He describes this "something more" in a variety of ways: A sense of atmosphere is conveyed; we feel that we have come close to experiencing a certain state or quality.

At the same time, there is frustration or tension in the structure of story—a frustration that story never fully overcomes. For a story is only a net with which we try to catch something else, something timeless, something more like a state or quality—a grand idea like homecoming, or reunion with a loved one, or the simple idea of otherness. But at the same time, story is narrative, involving temporal succession and plot. Hence the frustration. A story must involve a series of events. It must move on. But the thing itself—the thing we are seeking—is timeless. What we really seek to take hold of can never last in a story. And the storyteller is, therefore, doomed to frustration. The medium of the storyteller cannot grasp what is wanted. The medium, the story, is inherently temporal, yet the storyteller is trying to catch something that is not really a process at all—what Lewis calls *theme*. The art of the storyteller is to break through beyond the mere succession of particular experiences and to "catch" theme by means of plot.

What Lewis describes in his essay "On Stories" is essentially Lucy's experience on the island of the Dufflepuds. The story is a spell that brings "refreshment of the spirit." It brings one close to, if not directly into contact with, something entirely beyond time. But this all fades and is soon gone, for story is narrative. The spirit is both refreshed and frustrated because it has temporarily been drawn out of the constraints that time places upon us and, yet, has been so drawn by a literary form that is itself inherently temporal. Thus story—more than myth—unites the temporal and eternal as intimately as plot and theme.

Life as Narrative

This is Lewis's literary theory. Near the end of his essay "On Stories," however, Lewis makes a comment that carries us beyond literary considerations alone. "Shall I be thought whimsical," he writes, "if, in conclusion, I suggest that this internal tension in the heart of every story between the theme and the plot constitutes, after all, its chief resemblance to life?" Life, Lewis suggests, is frustrating in the same way a story is. "We grasp at a state and find only a succession of events in which the state is never embodied."

The author of a story uses temporal plot to catch a timeless theme, a temporal net to catch what is eternal. Life is the same sort of net, amenable to being understood within the narrative genre: a net of successive experiences seeking to catch something that is not temporal at all. Lewis's literary theory and his belief that the human heart is restless until it rests in God meet here.

What I have described might *almost* be said to be Lewis's metaphysic. Certain human experiences take us beyond—or almost beyond—the finite boundaries of life. But they never last. They pass us by and are gone. Still, they are clues, if we will follow them. How shall we do so? Not by constructing a completely explanatory theory that will itself attempt to be a timeless product, for our theories do not participate in the timelessness that we momentarily experience. The theorist is also a pilgrim; the theorist's own life has a narrative quality. As Stephen Crites has put it, every moment of experience is itself in tension, for memory (of the past) and anticipation (of the future) are the tension of every moment of experience.[9] Past and future, memory and anticipation, are themselves present. Hence, the present moment is "tensed." Tensed—and therefore filled with tension. As long as we remain within history we cannot escape that. We are limited to the present, yet in that very present both memory and anticipation serve as signals of transcendence.

Crites suggests that only narrative can contain the full temporality of our experience within a unity of form. And Lewis, I believe, is suggesting something similar. The human creature, made
for fellowship with God, can touch the Eternal but cannot (within
history) rest in it. For our experience is inherently narrative, relentlessly temporal. We are given no rest. The story moves on. And
hence, the creature who is made to rest in God is in this life best
understood as a pilgrim whose world is depicted in terms of the
Christian story. This may explain why stories are sometimes the
most adequate form for conveying the "feel" of human existence.

Most particularly, it is in stories that the quality—the feel—of
creatureliness may be most adequately conveyed. Lewis himself
suggests on one occasion that, "if God does exist, He is related to
the universe more as an author is related to a play than as one
object in the universe is related to another."[10] By way of illustration, he suggests that we think of looking for Shakespeare in his
plays. In one sense, Shakespeare is present at every moment in
every play—but not in the same way that Hamlet or King Lear is
present. Yet, we would not fully understand the plays if we did
not understand them in relation to Shakespeare, as the manifestation of his creative genius.

Even more important, narrative is the form that does justice to
the experience of creatures who are embodied spirits. Crites has
stressed the point that story does not isolate body and mind.
Lewis, likewise, seems to suggest that the narrative genre is most
appropriate for creatures who are finite, yet free. By trying to
catch in its net what is not temporal at all, story recognizes that we
are made to transcend our present condition. At the same time,
story is not just this grasping after a transcendent theme. Its
bodily structure, plot, always moves on. It is relentlessly temporal,
just as historical life is.

Because story gives no lasting rest, we may try to escape its
limitations. Lewis thinks we should not. He suggests that being a
pilgrim involves a willingness to accept the temporality of human

experience, a willingness to understand ourselves in terms of narrative structure and to accept the tension of the "tensed present."

In his essay on the narrative quality of experience, Crites describes two ways in which we may try to escape the temporality of our existence and find a rest in some false infinite of our own making. A reader of Lewis's *Pilgrim's Regress* [11] will recognize a striking similarity to the Northern and Southern ways that the pilgrim John must avoid as he travels the road. On the one hand, Crites believes, we may try to escape from narrative by abstraction. We may seek refuge in some theory that pretends to be timeless. Abstraction has an intellectual character, isolating mind from body. This is Lewis's "North," where all is arid, austere, bodiless, and finally sterile. The other attempted escape that Crites depicts is that of constriction: narrowing our attention to dissociated immediacies and disconnected particulars. In this case one assumes that feeling and sensation are irreducible in our experience. We accept our finite condition as the whole meaning of life and purchase timelessness by giving up the quest for the universal. We focus on the present, ignoring memory and anticipation, and do not see that particular experience calls us out beyond itself. This way is all body. It is Lewis's "South," where the pilgrim can find himself present at an orgy.

The first way is content to talk "about" the universal but gives up the quest to experience it. The second refuses to notice how particular experience calls us away from itself toward something that transcends all particularity. Lewis's pilgrim—an embodied spirit—is to eschew both ways of escape. His is to be a "feeling intellect."[12] Lewis says in his preface to *Pilgrim's Regress* that we were made "to be neither cerebral men nor visceral men, but Men"—things both rational and animal, creatures who are embodied and ensouled. We can neither abstract from the temporal flow of our experience nor reduce it to immediate experience without ignoring something important in our nature.

Story and Theology

If I have managed to convey my message at all successfully, its irony must certainly be clear, for in rather abstract fashion I have been suggesting that such abstract argument cannot successfully convey a quality like creatureliness. This raises, quite naturally, a problem for the theorist, in particular the theologian. If the quality of our experience through time is narrative, no theory—itself an abstraction from experience—can fully capture the truth of reality. There may be occasions when abstraction is important and necessary; nevertheless, it is no accident that Lewis writes stories instead of a *Summa*. The story is, on his account, the form most true to our experience. Its form makes clear that we grasp after what is not fully given.

There are certain features of our experience, essential to serious discussion of the Christian life, that cannot be adequately conveyed by theological treatment, however careful and precise. Thus, for example, Christians have commonly wanted to say that our commitment to God must be ours, freely and willingly given. Yet at the same time they have wanted to say that we are of ourselves incapable of making this commitment, that it must be "worked in us" by God's grace. Begin to abstract, isolate, and emphasize the divine activity and you end with irresistible grace, election of some to condemnation, and the suspicion that it is something of a sham to speak about our free and willing commitment. Begin to abstract, isolate, and emphasize our own free commitment and you end with Pelagianism, having made grace superfluous. Construct instead, however, a narrative of your own commitment—as Lewis does in *Surprised by Joy*—and it may make good sense to say *both* "I might not have made this commitment which I now freely and willingly make" *and* "I could not have so committed myself had I not been drawn by God, and it is really his doing." That is what believers are

likely to say in telling the story of how grace has abounded in their
own commitment. And within the narrative it seems to make sense to speak this
way. Similarly, Lewis writes of the Oedipus story, in which,
despite his efforts to avoid it, Oedipus kills his father and marries
his mother: "We have just had set before our imagination something that has always baffled the intellect: we have *seen* how
destiny and free will can be combined, even how free will is the
modus operandi of destiny. The story does what no theorem can
quite do. . . . It sets before us an image of what reality may well
be like at some more central region."[13] Or, to take an example
from the history of Christian thought, there are, I think, few
who would deny that St. Augustine's *Confessions* offers a more
compelling picture of the relation of creature and Creator—and
conveys better the paradox of a freely given commitment, elicited
solely by God's grace—than even the best of his more abstract
treatises on the grace of Christ and the predestination of the
saints. However important and necessary those treatises are in
certain contexts, they cannot convey the quality, the feel, of
creatureliness in the way the *Confessions* does.

But the treatises still *are* necessary in certain contexts. The theologian's task is not superfluous. In one of his brief essays Lewis
distinguishes nicely among ordinary language, scientific language,
and poetic language. He gives these illustrations of each:[14] (1) It
was very cold. (2) There were 13 degrees of frost. (3) "Ah, bitter
chill it was! The owl, for all his feathers was a-cold; The hare
limped trembling through the frozen grass. And silent was the
flock in wooly fold: Numb'd were the Beadsman's fingers." Theological language tries to bring to religion the technical precision of
scientific language. It is an attempt to provide what scientific
language offers in different contexts—a precise test that can end
dispute. It is language, as Lewis says, on which we can take action.[15] We can, for example, use it to guard against mistaken
understandings of our beliefs. But this is not the language the

believer naturally speaks, for such language cannot convey the quality of religious belief and experience. Believers, when questioned, are more likely to tell their story.

My theme is by now becoming familiar: Abstraction, however important, means a loss of immediacy, a loss of the sense of what it feels like to be (for example) a creature. And to see this theme in Lewis's writings is to begin to understand the wide appeal those writings continue to demonstrate. He appeals far less to theoretical argument than many of his readers (and critics) have imagined. Rather, he tells stories that expand the imagination and give one a world within which to live for a time. Like Lucy, the reader can almost forget that he is reading a story and can be "living in the story as if it were real." Lewis offers not abstract propositions for belief but the quality, the feel, of living in the world narrated by the biblical story. In stories we do not have to divide our treatment into separate loci—to talk first about the creature, then God (or first God, then the creature—on which distinction a good many theological arguments can be constructed). Instead, we are permitted to see God and the creature as they really are—in a narrative in which it makes little sense to think of human beings abstracted from either time and history or from the God-relation.

We may grant that there will still be something dissatisfying about this. The relentlessly temporal character of human life will tempt us to try to make our peace by separating theme and plot, dividing the feeling intellect into its parts. We may seek to view ourselves as all body, finding significance only in isolated present experiences (and regard the longing for something more as an absurdity). Or we may seek to view ourselves as all intellect, all free self-transcending person—as, in effect, one like God. But when we take either of these ways we will ultimately find ourselves talking about something other than human beings— creatures known properly only when known in relation to God, made for a destiny they cannot at present fully experience. The point is not, in the first instance, a religious one for Lewis. It is simply a claim about what rings true to our experience of what it means to be human. But, of course, it leads on to a religious claim. If we understand ourselves as creatures, we will recognize the narrative quality of our experience and may perhaps find a way to make peace with it.

The Christian Pilgrimage

How make that peace between the two sides of our nature? One might be drawn, as Lewis, always something of a Platonist, was, to turn to myth—to that permanent object of contemplation which, he believed, brings us into contact with a "more real" world. In myth one might transcend the limits of thought and "taste" the universal. However, this is a solution that temporarily eclipses but does not bridge the gap between time and eternity. We fall back from the mythic universal into our finitude—and have no truth to live by *there*. We want and need more, or so Lewis thinks. "In life and art both, as it seems to me, we are always trying to catch in our net of successive moments something that is not successive. Whether in real life there is any doctor who can teach us how to do it, so that at least either the meshes will become fine enough to hold the bird, or we be so changed that we can throw our nets away and follow the bird to its own country, is not a question for this essay." Thus Lewis writes in "On Stories." Elsewhere, however, he takes up that question and suggests that incarnation—for him the central turning point in the Christian story—surpasses even myth.[16] The Christian story affirms that in one human being that other and more real world has entered our history, that we need not transcend our finitude in order to find it.

The universal is particularized, located in time and space. The author has written himself into the play. As Augustine found the Word made flesh in the gospel but not in the Platonists, so here too Lewis has turned from myth to story and found the story that promises to satisfy the longing of the restless heart, while yet acknowledging, even affirming, the relentless temporality of a pilgrim existence.

3

The Place of Ethics in the Theological Task

If the human being is a strangely two-sided creature, a finite embodied person who is, nonetheless, made to rest in the eternal God, we should expect that there may be many occasions when we are perplexed about our moral responsibilities. In some moments love may demonstrate itself in a respect for the limits of human life; in other moments love may freely transgress a boundary once thought sacred. Because we cannot say that either stance—respect for, or transgression of, particular limits—is always the Christian stance, we may be tempted simply to proclaim purity of heart the law of Christian existence. We may say that motive—a heart that trusts and loves God—should alone count in moral evaluation. Then there would be no need for the kind of moral reflection still to come in later chapters of this book. No need to probe—and probe with a willingness to respect—the limits of the moral life. No need to chart, as best we are able, what fitting Christian decisions at the boundaries of human life might be. No need to consider with care how best to live within the most important bonds of human life—in marital and political communities. Nothing would matter but a right inner spirit, and we may quite properly doubt that it can be achieved through ethical reflection.

This is the *theological* challenge to succeeding chapters of this book—a challenge not to any particular conclusion but to the undertaking itself. And this challenge comes with an undeniably impressive pedigree. Among the twenty-seven proposals Luther set out for "improving the state of Christendom" in his appeal to the German nobility was one calling for university reform. In it he labeled Aristotle a "blind heathen teacher" and wrote that his *Ethics* was "the worst of all books. It flatly opposes divine grace and all Christian virtues. . . ."[1] What Luther had in mind is, I think, clear. For Aristotle, moral virtue is simply habit long continued. We become good people by doing good deeds—and gradually develop in ourselves the sort of character that *habitually* does the good deed. It is, therefore, important that we chart in considerable detail the nature of the virtues we seek to develop and the decisions and actions that will inculcate such habits of behavior. It is this sense that goodness can become our possession and can be developed through our own behavior that Luther described as flatly in opposition to divine grace. He, by contrast, emphasized a virtue (the righteousness of Christ) that is ours, though not our possession, and he held that truly virtuous deeds must be preceded by faith. A right inner spirit cannot be developed through doing the external deed. On the contrary, without that believing inner spirit no deed can really be good. What we need, therefore, is not moral reflection but a word that touches, transforms, and liberates the heart.

This challenge to ethics has still deeper and yet more impressive roots. St. Luke tells of the lawyer who came seeking to put Jesus to the test and, "desiring to justify himself," asked, "Who is my neighbor?" Countless preachers have observed that, in responding to him with the story of the Good Samaritan, Jesus does not really answer the lawyer's question but, instead, redirects the focus of his attention. What many of these preachers may have failed to note is that if we wish to engage in ethical reflection we will have to take our stand at the lawyer's side and press his question. That may be a risky and uncomfortable place to find oneself, but it is nevertheless where ethical reflection places us.

Jesus bypasses the lawyer's question in order to focus on the attitude of the heart. His own question—"Which of these three, do you think, proved neighbor to the man who fell among the thieves?" —is designed to uncover that attitude. It points the lawyer to what is undoubtedly the central religious question: his trust or lack of trust in God, and the effect this must have on his attitude toward the neighbor. But Jesus' story seems clear only because it is simple. Moral problems do not always come so simply packaged. "The most characteristic aspect of the Samaritan's behavior is that it is not of this world."[2] He is evidently going nowhere of any importance, since delaying his travel poses no problem. He evidently is bound by no previous obligations to others who might have a claim on his resources, since he writes a blank check for the innkeeper. This is not the way many problems strike us in a world in which all the good that ought to be done cannot be done. The lawyer's question may not be the most fundamental religious question, but it must be faced if we are to be faithful to that moment in the theological task that ethical reflection involves.

To be sure, the appropriateness of the theological challenge must not be denied. Hence, for example, the church's preaching ought certainly to be concerned chiefly with the question "How are we doing before God?" Theological ethics, however, is governed by the less profound but not unimportant question "What sort of persons should we be, and what ought we to do to serve our various neighbors?" It seeks to discern (as far as a faith seeking understanding can penetrate) the will for our finite, earthly life of the God who is gracious in Jesus Christ. In the law of that Lord one can delight.

The theological challenge to ethics may be put in terms of a question: How shall we picture the Christian life? We can see what is at stake here if we contrast two images of the Christian life—life as *journey* and as *dialogue*. We might think of the Christian life as a dialogue, with the Christian caught between the two voices with which God speaks: the demanding voice of law and the accepting voice of gospel. Hearing the law, we flee to the gospel. Hearing the gospel, we are set free to confront the requirements of the law. But hearing those demands, we must again flee to the gospel. Life is experienced as a dialogue between these two divine verdicts, and within human history one cannot escape that dialogue or progress beyond it. The Christian life goes, in a sense, nowhere; rather, it goes back and forth, back and forth. . . .

What could be the task of theological ethics within such a picture? Ethics can do no more than expose our condition before God, lay bare the state of our heart. We are either sinners under law or saints under grace. In fact, of course, we are both: sinner and saint simultaneously, caught in the dialogue between the two divine verdicts, needing always to hear the gospel anew in order that we may trust in the gracious rather than the condemning word of God. In this model of the Christian life as dialogue there can be no place for the notion of a sinner who is gradually coming to be (by God's grace) more and more a saint, no notion of progress in righteousness, of increasing conformity to God's will, of more God-pleasing service to the neighbor. No need, in short, for what ethics—as distinct from preaching—considers. No need to examine the freedom love gives or the limits it should respect.

We may also, by contrast, picture the Christian life as a journey: as the process by which God graciously transforms a sinner into a saint, as a pilgrimage (always empowered by grace) toward community with God. This picture directs our attention not simply to the proper inner spirit but to growth and progress along the way—to becoming the sort of person God wills us to be. The Christian life is pictured as going somewhere. It has, or ought to have, a definite shape. It finds in the divine will direction that need not be feared, guidance in which one can delight, encouragement to consider the shape love ought to take.

Each way of picturing the Christian life has its characteristic strengths and weaknesses. The image of life as journey makes place for the *truth about reality*—the truth that God intends to turn us into people who (gladly and without contrary inclination) do his will. Yet, by encouraging the pilgrim to concentrate on his own progress toward the goal, it makes possible the twin dangers of presumption and despair. We may forget that the entire journey, empowered by grace, leaves no room for self-confidence and boasting. Or, seeing little progress, we may begin to doubt whether God really intends to do this for us. The image of life as dialogue stays close to a central *truth of our experience*—that we are often unable to experience our lives as accepted by God and are, therefore, in constant need of hearing the renewing word of the gospel. Yet, precisely by adhering so steadfastly to this central insight about Christian experience, it may lead us to ignore an important element in the theological task: the need to explore the shape love should take in a responsible Christian life.

The tension between these two pictures of the Christian life cannot be overcome, nor should we try to overcome it.[3] Certainly we should not make place for theological ethics by the simple procedure of eliminating the picture of life as dialogue, for it stands as a constant and necessary reminder of the theological challenge to ethics. We can see, in a very simple way, both the problem and the profundity in this challenge if we think of the struggle every parent faces in seeking to "train up a child."

The problem: Why do parents worry about where their children go to school, about their playmates and peers, about the ways they use their free time, about the television shows they watch? They worry because all of us know that Aristotle was—at least to some extent—right. Moral virtue *is* habit long continued. The inner spirit is shaped and developed by the structures within which we live, the things we see and do daily. Only gradually do we become people who, for better or worse, can be depended upon to act in certain ways. It would be foolhardy just to speak the gospel to our children—relying on it alone to make them virtuous and shape their behavior, while paying no attention to their schools, their friends, the books they read. What happens quite often is that we do attend to all these other matters—but with a slightly bad conscience.

The profundity: There's a reason for that bad conscience. When all is said and done, what father wants to take full responsibility for shaping the character—much less the soul—of his child? What mother does not understand that her child's inner spirit is free and cannot simply be molded, however strenuous her efforts? Only God can bear such responsibility.

Taking both problem and profundity into account, we may conclude: We should probe as clearly as possible the limits of love and the shape of the Christian life. We should shape character, our own and that of others, as best we can. But we should also confess the character that we are to the only One who can see us whole. In the probing, shaping, and developing there is always need to separate the good from the bad; in the confessing, very little such need. Neither is fully safe without the other. And when both are taken seriously we will find developing what one writer has called "the hallmark of Christian character in all ages": "a combination of increasing humility and increasing achievement."[4] We should confess the self that we are, wholly and entirely, and wait to hear again the word that a virtue not ours is made our own. But then—whenever it should happen to be our calling—we should return with a glad heart to the lawyer's side, determined to explore the limits of love.

Part Two
The Beginning of Life

4

Babies Without Sex

Certain kinds of stories provide one of the most useful points of entry into the field of bioethics. The hatcheries of Aldous Huxley's *Brave New World,* which might at one time have seemed like a *reductio ad absurdum* of scientific progress, now begin to look remarkably like a vision of the not-too-distant future. As my starting point I want to take a few sentences from another story, C. S. Lewis's *That Hideous Strength,* which Lewis subtitled "A Modern Fairy-Tale for Grown-Ups." The title of the book is taken from a line in Sir David Lyndsay's *Ane Dialog,* a line that describes the tower of Babel: "The Shadow of that hyddeous strength / sax myle and more it is of length." And the book certainly evokes echoes of the Babel story. It concerns in large part the program of a National Institute of Co-ordinated Experiments (N.I.C.E)—an ambitious attempt to control and shape nature.

At one point in the story, Mark Studdock learns from Filostrato—a member of N.I.C.E. who strikes the reader as slightly mad—that the N.I.C.E. program involves the destruction of all organic life. Filostrato anticipates, for example, a day—a far more rational day—when artificial, metal trees will replace the real ones. Then, if we tire of a tree in one place, we simply move it elsewhere. "It never dies. No leaves to fall, no twigs, no birds building nests, no muck and mess."[1] Applied to human beings, Filostrato's theory is striking. "What," he asks, "are the things that most offend the dignity of man?" And he answers, "Birth and breeding and death."[2] Organic life, having done its work in producing mind, can now be eliminated. Death can be conquered, and reproduction need no longer involve copulation.

Filostrato may be mad, but he is not crazy. Indeed, by his own lights and the lights of some in our day, he is eminently rational. At the very least, he provides a good starting point for us when we consider one of those features of human existence that Filostrato found most offensive: birth and breeding. The biblical story depicts a world within which a rational view of birth and breeding may be somewhat different from Filostrato's.

The Meaning of Creatureliness

To think of human life under the rubric of story or narrative is more than a useful device. It is essential for capturing some of what it means to call ourselves *creatures*. The biblical story recounts a pilgrimage of those who are made to rest in the Eternal One, but who—made from the dust of the ground—journey toward that rest through a material, fleshly world bounded by the forms of space and time. For such pilgrims life is a bundle of successive experiences, none of which can give purpose or unity to the whole, all of which do not in themselves add up to the fellowship with God for which we are created. We can put the point in Reinhold Niebuhr's terms: Human beings stand "at the juncture of nature and spirit."[3] That is to say, our rootedness in the biological realm of natural necessity places certain limits upon us—limits that ought to be respected by anyone who takes seriously the embodied character of human existence. At the same time, however, we are creatures made for a goal that transcends the limits of human history, and we therefore indefinitely transcend the limits of nature.

Human beings are finite yet free. And there is no better way to capture this duality than in terms of narrative structure. A story may have a timeless theme, but it must also—in order to be a story—involve a succession of events. Hence, there is a certain duality built into narrative structure. The medium of the story is inherently temporal, yet this succession of events is held together within a unity of form, a unity that offers the reader a kind of timeless whole. Thus, St. Augustine, reflecting on the mystery of time, noted that both memory (of the past) and expectation (of the future) are *present* in our experience.

> No one, of course, can deny that the future does not yet exist. But nevertheless there is in the mind already the expectation of the future. No one can deny that the past no longer exists. But nevertheless there is still in the mind the memory of the past. No one can deny that the present time has no extension, since it passes in a flash. But nevertheless our attention (our "looking at") is something constant and enduring, and through it what is to be proceeds into what has been.

Augustine suggests the analogy of reciting a psalm. Before beginning, one's expectation embraces the whole psalm. As one recites, those parts that have been spoken fall into the past, into memory. "So the life of this action of mine is extended in two directions— toward my memory, as regards what I am about to recite. But all the time my attention . . . is present and through it what was future passes on its way to become past." At which point Augustine suggests that a human life and the whole of human history are best understood in terms of such a narrative structure—embracing past and future within the unity of a story. "It is true also of the whole of a man's life, of which all his actions are parts. And it is true of the whole history of humanity, of which the lives of all men are parts."[4]

Duality—but not dualism—is the mark of narrative, and, in particular, of the biblical narrative. We may be free spirits made to transcend all that is finite and to rest in God, but we are just as truly bodies subject to the relentless temporality of human experience. Hence, the present moment is always, in Stephen Crites's felicitous phrase, a "tensed present."[5] There are limits that ought to bind us, that we ought not to seek to transcend, but it is difficult to specify these in advance. We can hardly say that to transcend any of the limits that time, space, and biological necessity place upon us is wrong, for it is precisely this transcending that manifests human freedom. Neither can we assume that freedom is the only essential feature of our being and approve every step beyond old limits simply because such a step manifests the self-transcending power of human freedom. For any particular step may be the one step we ought not to take.

We are creatures who stand at the *juncture* of nature and spirit, always threatened by an unbiblical dualism that would tear these two asunder. It is the primal sin of pride to refuse to recognize any sense of limits, to attempt to be as God. But it is also sinful—though perhaps not in quite so fundamental a sense—simply to acquiesce in the limits imposed upon us and to refuse the call of freedom. That is the sin of sloth: a failure to affirm, develop, and rejoice in an integral part of our created nature, human freedom.

Creaturely Procreation

We can begin to press these somewhat abstract reflections in the direction of bioethics if we consider what Lewis Thomas has noted about the deeply buried origins of our word "hybrid." It comes from the Latin *hybrida,* the name for the offspring of a wild boar and a domestic sow. But in its more distant origins the word, as Thomas puts it, "carries its own disapproval inside."[6] Its more distant ancestor is the Greek *hubris,* insolence against the gods. That is, buried somewhere in the development of our language is a connection between two beings unnaturally joined together and human usurping of the prerogatives of the gods. Hence, as Thomas summarizes his excursion into etymology: "This is what the word has grown into, a warning, a code word, a shorthand signal from the language itself: if man starts doing things reserved for the gods, deifying himself, the outcome will be something worse for him, symbolically, than the litters of wild boars and domestic sows were for the ancient Romans."[7] But that is only one side of the matter, for Thomas can also write in a provocative paragraph:

> Is there something fundamentally unnatural, or intrinsically wrong . . . in the ambition that drives us all to reach a comprehensive understanding of nature, including ourselves? I cannot believe it. It would seem to be a more unnatural thing . . . for us to come on the same scene endowed as we are with curiosity . . . and then for us to do nothing about it or, worse, to try to suppress the questions. This is the greater danger for our species, to try to pretend . . . that we do not need to satisfy our curiosity. . . .[8]

Lewis Thomas is not a theologian, but—except that, like a good modern, he regards sloth as more dangerous than pride—he has grasped the duality of our creatureliness. Simply to fall back into our finitude and ignore the lure of new possibilities is itself a denial of our nature. And yet, one never knows when the creation of the hybrid may be an act of hubris. Is there any way to draw the line?

Artificial reproduction is now a fact in our world. To concentrate on it for a moment is to focus on "birth and breeding," one of those elements Filostrato found so offensive in ordinary human life. We can produce babies without sex by means of in vitro fertilization followed by reimplantation (test-tube babies), through the use of surrogate mothers, through artificial insemination, through embryo transfer (in which a fertilized ovum is removed from the uterus of one woman and implanted in that of another). The day is at hand when a child can be born with five "parents": the man who donated the sperm, the woman who donated the egg, the woman who received the embryo after sperm and egg were united in the laboratory and carried the fetus to term, and the (probably infertile) couple who commissioned the process and will undertake to raise the child.

This separation of genetic, gestational, and social parentage raises many questions that affect our sense of what it means to be human. That a child may be conceived *in order* to be given away should be deeply disturbing. But it is perhaps not surprising that as we gradually learn to think of procreation as reproduction—as a process of manufacture—we should also learn to think of the child as a product or commodity whose usefulness can be measured (and even priced). That the creation of new life should deliberately be separated from the marital union or, at least, from the fleshly act by which husband and wife fully give themselves and express their love is also disturbing—a further sign of our alienation from the natural world, of our tendency to make of love only a motive that can take shape in any way.

But such questions only drive us back to the most fundamental problem: the relation of freedom and finitude in the human being. What, from that perspective, shall we say about making babies without sex? We cannot avoid remarking what a striking manifestation of human freedom this is. The manufacture of human life in a test tube surpasses an old limit that seemed rooted in our finitude, in the world of biological necessity, and surpasses it in a way earlier generations could scarcely have dreamed possible. But at the same time—and without taking that back—we must also see that this may be an exercise of freedom that eliminates something fundamentally human from the act of begetting: the way in which (as with the animals) it involves our bodies, not just our minds, the way it has been connected to the act in which human beings are present most fully and give themselves most completely to another.[9]

The old limit is transcended, yet it was that very limit that recognized procreation as a bodily, fleshly act—that recognized that we human beings are not just mind but also body, not just spirit but also nature, creatures whose most creative act takes place in the loins rather than the intellect. When we make babies without sex we use our freedom to destroy something just as essential to created human nature as freedom. We transform the act of begetting into manufacture of a product. (And we should not be surprised if "quality control" becomes an essential part of the process.) Only an exceedingly dualistic age could do this. And, we might add, only a vision no longer shaped by narrative—and, in particular, by the biblical narrative that recognizes both the transcendent goal toward which we strain *and* the limits of our temporal condition—could foster and nourish that dualism.

Procreation first became reproduction in our thoughts—only then in our deeds. That historical shift depends not just on the development of new technological possibilities but on a dualism that can find no integral connection between body and person. This historical transformation seems eminently rational, of course, just as Filostrato's plan for artificial trees does when viewed within a certain context; however, it is in the most fundamental sense irrational. It is all mind and no body and cannot, therefore, be adequate to creatures such as we are.

5

The Fetus as Parasite and Mushroom

In one of the most widely anthologized of recent articles about abortion, Judith Jarvis Thomson has provided a defense of abortion that, she contends, does not rely on denying human status to the fetus-to-be-aborted.[1] A great deal of the persuasive force of her argument depends, I am inclined to think, on two analogies she uses. My purpose is to reflect on these analogies and to suggest that they are very strange indeed. The first of Thomson's analogies reflects an excessively individualistic notion of human personhood, a notion oblivious to the bonds that tie us to one another. The second expresses (but does not reflect upon) a person-body dualism. Together these analogies subtly distort the matter under discussion and manifest an insensitivity to the human character of birth and motherhood.

I will not try to argue here that all abortion is wrong nor even provide the beginnings of an argument to that effect. I will also not try to settle the difficult question of the point in time at which we have among us a new life, a new individual human being. These are important questions and necessary for any full-fledged treatment of abortion. They are not, however, my primary concern here. It is Thomson's images, not her arguments, upon which I focus.

Thomson herself grants for the sake of argument that the fetus is a person from the moment of conception (p. 48). Her concern is to suggest that opponents of abortion have tended to assume that, once this was established, the argument against abortion was finished. She, on the contrary, is puzzled about the move from the affirmation of the personhood of the fetus to the conclusion that the fetus can claim rights against the mother or that abortion is not morally permissible. She thinks that opponents of abortion pass over this problem much too quickly. In this she may well be correct, though it is worth noting even here that there is something a little strange about her case. If the fetus is a person—which we are granting for the sake of the discussion—then surely the burden of proof is on the side of those who deny that rights may properly be ascribed to it or who advocate taking its life. Thomson talks as if there were something unusual about this, whereas I should think it rather clear. It is not at all surprising that opponents of abortion should have assumed that persons have rights (and, most basically, a right to life), nor that they should have called upon others to protect these rights. It is not surprising that opponents of abortion should have confined their efforts largely to discussing when human life begins and to criticizing various proposed defenses of aborting such lives. To do that, of course, even to do it successfully, is not to show that no such defense is possible. But it is a perfectly understandable procedure if one assumes that—in the absence of forceful arguments to the contrary—one human life (even that of the fetus) is entitled to as much protection as another. That Thomson seems to distribute the burden of proof wrongly from the outset is itself cause for wonder.

The Fetus as Parasite

Suppose we grant that the fetus is a person, how then might we argue that abortion is, nevertheless, morally permissible? Thomson suggests that the mother's right to decide what happens to her body is stronger than the fetus's right to life—or, at least, that the mother is under no obligation to permit the fetus to continue to grow within her body. She grants, of course, that in some instances it would be morally reprehensible for the mother to abort the fetus. She speaks of Good Samaritans, Splendid Samaritans, and so forth. But these do more than their duty. There is in no case an *obligation* not to abort or a justified rights-claim on the part of the fetus. At this point we may consider her first analogy: that of the unconscious violinist.

You are asked to suppose this case: There is a famous violinist suffering from a fatal ailment, and you alone have the right type of blood to help him. One night the Society of Music Lovers kidnaps you and plugs the violinist's circulatory system into yours. In this way the violinist can (for the amount of time needed to save his life) live off your system. Your kidneys can be used to extract poisons from his system as well as from yours. You wake up in the morning and find yourself in bed with the unconscious violinist, his system plugged into yours. And the question is whether it would be morally wrong for you or anyone else to unplug you, when such action would certainly mean the death of the violinist.

The force of the analogy is to present the opponent of abortion with a dilemma. If he says, "Once (innocent) life exists we should not directly take it," he seems committed to leaving himself plugged into the violinist for as long as necessary. If, on the other hand, he claims that the cases are markedly dissimilar in that he did not voluntarily consent to be plugged into the violinist, his case against abortion in certain kinds of situations (e.g., cases of rape) seems to collapse.

The one good thing I can think of to say for this analogy and the dilemma Thomson generates on the basis of it is that it may help us see why abortion in cases of pregnancy resulting from rape *is* a very special and different matter. I am not, however, certain that Thomson always sees *why* this is so. She seems to think that rape is an exception *just as* a pregnancy that required the mother to spend nine months in bed would be an exception (pp. 49f.). That she can run together pregnancy resulting from forcible intercourse with other cases is nothing short of remarkable. This shows that rape is an exception in her thinking only because it seems to impose a special burden for which the mother did not volunteer.

Thomson seems oblivious to what is surely more important than the fact that the mother did not "invite" this fetus in— namely, the nature of the relationship in which the fetus was conceived, a relationship that strikes most of us as not only less than human but inhuman. This same blind spot is manifested later in her essay when Thomson suggests that a woman who became pregnant as a result of rape ought to carry the child to term if the pregnancy lasted only an hour (p. 60). In that case, the implication seems to be, the burden (though not volunteered for) would not be great enough to justify a refusal. Yet, even in such a case the relationship in which the fetus had been conceived would be one repugnant to our sense of humanity. The woman's body would have been forcibly used as a means for someone else's pleasure in a relationship devoid of genuine giving and receiving. Unless we think persons are not present in their bodies (as, we shall see, there is some reason to believe Thomson thinks), this means that not only the woman's body but her person has been used in an inhuman manner. One would, however, never guess any of this from Thomson's argument.

More important than this, however, is the way the analogy forces one to picture the fetus: as parasite. And, of course, there is no doubt that the fetus does for nine months live off the mother and make use of the mother's circulatory and waste-disposal systems. But shall we acquiesce in this picture of the fetus as parasite? Or shall we suggest that it subtly distorts the entire discussion? The latter seems to be the case.

There is, in the conception and growth of the fetus in its mother's womb, a striking act of creativity. This very same act witnesses as well to the self-spending that such creativity requires. That for nine months the child lives within (and, indeed, off) the mother provides a paradigm of human dependence and, we might also say, vicariousness. There is no human being who has not been so bound to others from the moment of his birth. For Thomson this is just so much biology, the relationship between mother and child being merely a biological one with no special human significance (p. 65). In her account, human significance seems to enter only when an act of will takes place, when the parent recognizes or acknowledges the child and thereby takes responsibility for it. Whatever it is that characterizes our humanity evidently has more relation to seeing ourselves as "isolated principles of will"[2] than as embodied creatures.

And yet, it is not impossible to think differently about the fact that the fetus lives off its mother. We may see there a sign of what is truly human: an inescapable witness to the self-spending that human life requires and to the bonds of vicarious dependence that encompass the lives of us all. We may see there a sign—indeed, more than that, an embodiment—of the fact that we *do* live off others who never invited us to do so or granted us any rights thereto. And we may even find there an invitation to recognize that we cannot, without forfeiting our humanity, turn from the giving which is the other side of that receiving.

The first thing we notice, therefore, when we begin with Thomson to picture the fetus as parasite is the striking individualistic bias of this viewpoint. Vicariousness is to her simply a burden, not an essential part of creative human love. Perhaps then we ought to examine this picture of the fetus as parasite, reflect upon it a little more.

The womb is the natural environment of the fetus. We expect to find it there. We expect to find it nourished by and living off the mother. We expect, in short, that it will be dependent in this way. Yet, if we want to claim that there is moral significance to be discerned here—that here we may learn something about the proper shape of human life—we will have to say more than this. For could we not say much the same of any parasite that lives off its host? Is not the host its natural environment? Do we not expect to find the parasite dependent in this way? Will we not find both fetus living off mother and parasite living off host in nature? Why, then, should the cases be different?

"For most creatures," Annie Dillard writes, "being parasitized is a way of life."[3] We could, she suggests, write a "lives of the parasites" that would be a kind of "hellish hagiography," the devil's *summa theologica*.[4] Parasitism may, though I think it should not, be defined simply in terms of dependency. On this sort of definition "the essential criterion of parasitism is dependency, the loss of freedom to live an independent existence. . . ."[5] Such a definition may be too broad, however, since it might with some justification be taken to apply to almost anything in nature understood as an interconnected system. It is perhaps better to define parasitism more narrowly as "a type of symbiosis in which two different kinds of organism habitually associate with one another, to the detriment of one and the benefit of the other."[6] Annie Dillard's book is a gold mine of hair-raising descriptions of parasitism, if one is interested in examples. She writes at one point of an order of parasitic insects called "stylops."

Stylops parasitize diverse other insects such as leaf hoppers, ants, bees, and wasps. The female spends her entire life inside the body of her host, with only the tip of her bean-shaped body protruding. She is a formless lump, having no wings, legs, eyes, or antennae; her vestigial mouth and anus are tiny, degenerate, and nonfunctional. She absorbs food—her host—through the skin of her abdomen, which is "inflated, white, and soft."[7]

Considering this and other like "natural" phenomena, Dillard is moved to ask: "Are my values then so diametrically opposed to those that nature preserves?" and "Is human culture with its values my only real home after all?" [8]

Perhaps the fetus in the mother's womb is just one more example of such parasitism. Why should we not picture it that way? The first thing that needs to be said is that we certainly can picture it that way. The second is that we need not do so. Nature provides us with countless examples of dependence. But nature's book must be read.

It is possible to think that some examples of dependence that nature presents us are corruptions or perversions of a principle that is rightly exemplified in others. Thus, the fact that the fetus lives off the mother while in her womb may be of enormous human significance and tell us much about what is appropriate to our natures. We may say with Marcel that "a family is not created or maintained as an entity without the exercise of a fundamental generosity." [9] That the parasite lives off the host demonstrates only that the principle of vicariousness can be distorted. Such an insight lay behind St. Augustine's privative theory of evil. When he says that evil has no independent existence and that it can exist only as a corruption of what is good, he is both giving us a reading of nature's book and asserting the priority of goodness. [10]

From this perspective, while granting that the fetus is in some respects like a parasite, we may come to see that the two are nevertheless quite different phenomena. They are ordered toward different ends. The analogy of the fetus as parasite fails to take note of the fact that parasitism is not a method of procreation. Creatures that are parasites have other—sometimes asexual—means of reproduction. To construct an analogy that invites us to picture the fetus as a parasite is, therefore, to misplace the phenomenon. Parasitism is different from procreation of one's kind. Furthermore, the fetus in the womb is moving toward a stage when it will attain a kind of independence relative to its earlier condition. But parasitism, on the other hand, "involves a gradual and progressive adaptation on the part of the parasite, and recovery of an independent status becomes increasingly difficult."[11] We may recall the stylops. The vicariousness of which the fetus provides a paradigm is strikingly creative—oriented not toward degenerative dependence but toward new life that will be able to give as it has received. Rightly ordered, vicariousness is meant to be creative and life-giving.

I have put the point in Augustinian terms. Augustine's belief, of course, had some theological roots. He knew and believed a story that spoke of nature as a good thing now corrupted. It gave him warrant, therefore, to expect that he might find in nature a relationship that could be exemplified in both good and bad ways. But we can also put the matter in slightly less theological terms. That the parasite lives off its host and the child off its mother are both natural in the sense that observation and inspection find both in nature. But in that sense, of course, nothing can be unnatural; whatever upon inspection we find simply *is* exhibited as part of nature, and corruption cannot exist. When we read nature's book, however, it is possible to say that some acts or conditions exemplify vicariousness in its natural—i.e., rightly ordered—state. Some sorts of dependence are appropriate to the sorts of creatures we are, even as some are corruptions of our nature.

We acknowledge this to be the case when we say that the womb of the mother is the natural environment of the fetus. It is quite appropriate for our natures that we should find the fetus there. Indeed, we think it of great human significance. How one proves to the skeptic that it *is* of such significance I am not at all sure. It is always possible to refuse to distinguish one example of vicariousness from another. It is possible to grant no significance to the fact that the dependence of the fetus is part of a creative act oriented toward new life. We certainly *can* think of individuals as isolated and refuse to grant that creation of new life has its origin in an act of self-spending that ought to be pronounced good. Therefore, I am uncertain how, in any strong sense, to prove what I have argued for. And yet, to think that it needs to be proven is already to imagine that we can think of human beings in isolation, apart from this relation of vicarious dependence. It is, in short, to imagine that we can think of them as other than human. We cannot, of course, prevent Thomson from adopting an angle of vision that pictures the fetus as if it were a parasite. But when she does this she is no longer discussing anything that we understand to be a human being. Hence, her analogy is subtly distorting. We cannot heed *both* it *and* her prior affirmation that she will grant from the outset that the fetus is a human being. The analogy asks us to picture the fetus as a parasite, and, though we can do that, we cannot do it while simultaneously thinking of the fetus as a human being.

When we see the parasite living off its host, we see a corrupt imitation of something that in itself exhibits right order; namely, the dependence of the fetus on its mother and the vicarious character of human life to which it witnesses. That we should find both in a world in which, as Augustine put it, pride perversely copies the work of love need not particularly surprise us. Thomson's picture of the fetus as parasite misses the human significance of vicarious dependence within love—and in so doing betrays the individualistic bias of her argument.

The Fetus as Mushroom

There is a later stage in Thomson's argument that also needs examination. In the course of broadening her defense of abortion to include within its scope many cases in which the mother willingly and knowingly risked pregnancy, she provides us with a new analogy. We are now asked to suppose that people-seeds drift about in the air like pollen, and if you open your windows, one may drift in and take root in your carpets or upholstery. You don't want children, so you fix up your windows with fine mesh screens, the very best you can buy. As can happen, however, and on very, very rare occasions does happen, one of the screens is defective, and a seed drifts in and takes root. (p. 59)

I label this picture "the fetus as mushroom" as a way of recalling that the imagery is scarcely original with Thomson. In his *De Cive,* Thomas Hobbes suggests that we "consider men as if but even now sprung out of the earth, and suddenly, like mushrooms, come to full maturity, without all kind of engagement to each other."[12] Part of the point of the analogy for Thomson is to suggest that parents may or may not, as they wish, take responsibility for children resulting from contraceptive failure. If, however, the opponent of abortion must wriggle a bit when claiming that cases of pregnancy resulting from rape differ in no special way from other pregnancies, surely we ought to wonder at least as much about an argument that suggests that pregnancy resulting from contraceptive failure is involuntary in a way similar to pregnancy resulting from rape.

But to focus on the analogy of fetus as mushroom: What angle of vision does it invite us to adopt? When the fetus is pictured this way, the biological relationship between mother (or parents) and child is of no special significance. It does not involve us personally in any important way, and we are essentially individuals isolated from one another. This is, I think, just one example of the very disembodied concept of a person that floats around Thomson's essay. There are strange dualisms scattered throughout it, not least of which is the talk about the mother's body as a house she owns. Indeed, we might say that here the analogies merge. Individualism and dualism feed one another as the fetus is conceived of both as parasite and mushroom.

Had Shakespeare known what Thomson knows we might have been bereft of some immortal lines. For, when Romeo creeps into Juliet's courtyard and she comes onto the balcony, Shakespeare places into Juliet's mouth the philosophy of Thomson and Hobbes:

> O Romeo, Romeo! Wherefore art thou Romeo?
> Deny thy father and refuse thy name!
> Or if thou wilt not, be but sworn my love,
> and I'll no longer be a Capulet.
> . . . .
> 'Tis but thy name that is my enemy.
> . . . .
> . . . O, be some other name![13]

But, of course, Shakespeare knows—and we are to know—that this philosophy is false. Juliet would have us pretend that we are "even now sprung out of the earth, and suddenly, like mushrooms, come to full maturity, without all kind of engagement to each other." It is not surprising that the story of one who believes that should be a tragedy. Romeo is a Montague and Juliet a Capulet. But is that not mere biology? Evidently not, for mere biology does not seem to have a part in the play. Romeo can no more deny his father or his name than Juliet can cease to be a Capulet. Their names help to fix their respective personal histories.

Thomson's picture of the fetus as mushroom would deny human, personal significance to a biological relationship that marks each of us. And here again we encounter the same problem in trying to adopt Thomson's angle of vision. We can think of creatures like the mushrooms her analogy suggests. But we cannot think of them in the terms her argument purports to grant: as human beings. For she has abstracted them from one of the relationships that importantly characterize our humanity.

My purpose in this chapter can, on the one hand, be construed

very modestly indeed. I have merely tried to explain why it is that
Thomson's defense of abortion appears to distort the issue almost
beyond recognition. But, of course, the issues raised are really far
from modest, and they involve questions beyond the scope of a
single chapter. The burden of my concern has been to ask how we are to
discuss this issue. Thomson does not seem to me to discuss it in
the terms she says she will grant. One does not know how she
pictures a human being or what she thinks a person is. At times
it seems that one cannot be a person unless some other person
(how identified?) confers that status. At other times it seems that
a person is a kind of disembodied, volitional agent. To subscribe
to such views is, I believe, mistaken. But, then, how shall we
discuss abortion? What shall we take Thomson to mean when
she says she will assume that the fetus is a person? Her analogies
seem to suggest that persons are, in important ways, like parasites and mushrooms. Evidently she thinks it illuminating to
picture human beings in that way. I confess that I do not. Thus,
as least from certain perspectives, an argument like Thomson's
must appear to be a sham, denying in its content what it pro-
fesses to grant in its initial assumptions and thereby subtly lead-
ing the discussion astray.

6

Against Abortion

For anyone troubled by the permissive attitude toward abortion in our society, the traditional position of Roman Catholic moral theology is likely to appear inviting. And, indeed, it would be hard to deny that, from the normative perspective of one who *is* deeply disturbed by an easy acceptance of abortion, Catholic moral theology has proved far more satisfactory than most Protestant ethical reflection.[1] In limiting permissible abortions to cases where life conflicts with equal life, Catholic thought, though unacceptable to many in our society, will be congenial to the Protestant who also believes that fetal life is human life and that all human lives are entitled to equal respect. Yet, the Catholic position on abortion, relying as it does on the difficult concept of indirect killing and the related double-effect category, presents the Protestant with certain problems. Furthermore, in suggesting that even in certain conflict cases we must stand aside and permit nature to take its course, traditional Catholic moral reflection runs contrary to some of our most fundamental intuitions and seems to consider insufficiently the fact that the "nature" we know is disordered and cannot be equated with "creation" as it comes from the hand of the Creator.

On the other hand, the great advantage of Catholic teaching is that those abortions that it does countenance are strictly limited to a carefully circumscribed set of cases—thereby avoiding the danger of justifying more than we originally intended. The Protes-

tant, if he forgoes concepts such as indirect killing, is in danger of
finding no way to limit the death-dealing blow to cases where life
conflicts with equal life. It is not surprising, therefore, to find a
Protestant ethicist like Paul Ramsey using double-effect reasoning
to explain why Christian love should lead to a restrictive position
on abortion.[2] Nevertheless, it is worth asking whether a Protestant position can be developed that can restrict the number of
permissible abortions on other grounds. To sketch such a position
is the purpose of this chapter.[3]

The Traditional Catholic Position

Though the Catholic position, having developed over centuries, is
in some ways enormously complex, I will concern myself only with
its core elements. At its center the Catholic view accomplishes two
goals: (1) It affirms the equal value of every human being and
therefore the right of every human life to protection; and (2) it
finds a way (by means of the concept of indirect killing) to permit
intervention in some but not all cases of parity conflicts of life with
life. What is important—and deserving of great respect—is the way
in which (1) and (2) are held together in a coherent position. Those
interventions that are permitted are understood in such a way that
they do not call into question the fundamental premise (equal
respect for human lives) on which the position is founded. The
alternative I am seeking would be a view that accepted (1) but
found a substitute for (2)—a substitute that would permit us to
intervene in all (not just some) conflict cases but that would, like
the Catholic position, countenance intervention in all cases where
life conflicts with equal life and would, apart from such instances,
strictly limit the permitted interventions.

The first element in the Catholic position grows out of several beliefs that are, or ought to be, common Christian affirmations. All human life comes from God, is endowed by him with worth and dignity, and ought to be respected and protected.

The affirmation that all human life comes from God is connected to the imperative enjoining equal protection of human lives by the rule that St. Thomas describes as the fundamental natural law: Do good and avoid evil. This imperative, combined with a belief that life is God's gift, requires that we both seek to preserve life and refrain from direct killing of innocent life. Nevertheless, this fundamental natural law actually involves two precepts: "Do good" and "avoid evil." And there is a sense in which the second of these has priority over the first.[4]

We are to do all the good we can, but that means all the good we morally can. It is conceivable, in other words, that certain acts that are intrinsically evil (and which therefore violate the precept "avoid evil") might, at the same time, benefit our fellows (and therefore fulfill the precept "do good"). Should any such case arise, Catholic moral theology has traditionally maintained that the negative precept takes precedence over the positive. We cannot do evil that good may come of it. We are to do all the good we morally can, not simply all the good we can.

A similar point has sometimes been made by philosophers in terms of the distinction between duties of perfect and imperfect obligation. Duties of perfect obligation (like the negative precept) always bind. Duties of imperfect obligation (like the positive precept) enjoin us to act in certain ways but do not specify the precise circumstances under which we are to do so. Hence, my duty to be beneficent is a duty of imperfect obligation. It enjoins certain actions but permits me to decide the times and places in which I will carry out my beneficence. On the other hand, a duty of perfect obligation—e.g., the duty to refrain from inflicting needless suffering—always binds in all circumstances.

In Catholic moral theology the suggestion that we are to do all the good we morally can has sometimes been made, not by stressing that negative precepts take priority over positive or by explicating the distinction between duties of perfect and imperfect obligation, but by distinguishing between moral and physical evil. To say that we cannot do evil that good may come of it is not to say that we could never cause certain physical evils in order to achieve some good effects. It is *moral* evil that cannot be done even for the sake of achieving good results. The difficulty the Protestant almost instinctively feels with this distinction is that it inevitably strikes one as an attempt to "keep our hands clean" and refrain from sin even if the price is also refraining from service to the neighbor. I want to suggest, however, that something like this distinction ought to be part of any Christian ethic and that it can be correctly understood. To say that (moral) evil should not be done even to achieve (physical) good simply means in this context that the precept "avoid evil" retains its priority.

Consider an example taken from Philippa Foot, a British moral philosopher.[5] She suggests that we consider the following two cases and ponder our reactions to them:

(1) You are the driver of a runaway railroad engine. You can steer only from one narrow track onto another, no other options being open to you. On one of these tracks five men are working, and on the other one man is working. What should you do?

(2) You are a public official faced with rioters demanding that a culprit be found for a certain crime. The rioters have taken five hostages, whom they threaten to put to death unless the culprit is punished. Since the real culprit is unknown, it is suggested that you frame one innocent person, thereby saving the five hostages and having to execute only the one innocent man. What should you do?

Intuitively we are likely to think that in case (1) we ought to steer toward the track where only one man is working but that in case (2) we ought not to frame one innocent man in order to save the five. Yet, in both cases we might say that the consequences are the same—the numbers certainly are. Why think that five ought to be saved in case (1) and not also in case (2)?

Foot suggests that we distinguish between positive and negative duties (which is nothing more, really, than her way of distinguishing the two halves of the injunction to "do good and avoid evil"). Negative duties enjoin us to refrain from injuring other persons in a variety of ways. Positive duties enjoin us to bring aid, also in a variety of ways. Foot's crucial assertion, which is in agreement with the description of Catholic moral theology given above, is that if a negative and a positive duty conflict the negative duty has the stronger claim upon us.

This distinction helps to show what is at stake in our differing intuitions with respect to Foot's two examples. In case (1) we have a conflict between negative duties—harming either one or five men. In such a circumstance, Foot thinks we can do little more than save the larger number of men. But in case (2) we have a conflict between a negative and a positive duty—the duty to refrain from injuring the innocent man who might be framed and the duty to bring aid, if we can, to the five hostages. In such a case the negative duty, Foot suggests, has the stronger claim upon us. We ought always, of course, to try to bring aid if we can. But, as we have seen, that means "if we morally can," and the violation of a negative duty is not an acceptable means to choose for fulfilling a positive duty. This may help us to see that it is not simply a question of permitting physical evil in order to avoid moral evil—a formulation that seems semantically to smack of protecting our moral purity and keeping our hands clean, or that suggests that physical evil is totally unrelated to our moral failure. Instead, we can see that here we are simply trying to understand the relation between several kinds of moral obligations. The agent is not just trying to keep his moral integrity. Rather, he is asking what fidelity to the various neighbors and their claims upon us would require.

We can apply the distinction to the matter of abortion and then consider what theological backing we might offer in support of Foot's philosophy and our intuitions. By distinguishing negative from positive duties and giving greater moral weight to the former, we can, it seems, limit permissible abortions to cases of conflict of life with equal life. We will have to refrain from injuring the fetus in order to assist family-planning projects (even those of relatively impoverished families, who certainly ought to be aided in other ways that do not violate negative duties); we will have to refrain from injuring the fetus in order to satisfy a whim of the mother, even one grounded in an alleged right to privacy; we will have to refrain from injuring a disabled or retarded fetus whose care would place a heavy burden upon its family; and so forth. In all such cases the duty not to harm the fetus will take precedence over our other obligations to bring both serious and trivial aid to others involved.

This sort of distinction is not without theological warrant. Why is it that negative duties should carry greater moral weight than positive duties? It is, I suggest, because from the perspective of Christian theology moral agents always remain *creatures*. The creature is one who understands her life and action in terms of a story God is telling, a story that begins in the primeval creative utterance and that will one day, having reached its appointed conclusion, end. Only the Author of the drama is in a position to specify clearly the ultimate significance of the roles particular creatures are called upon to play.[6] Only He may fully see how the various roles make up a coherent whole. The creature who plays her role may be uncertain of its final significance or importance; she may even be uncertain whether the story is now in its final chapters or whether the plot is just beginning to get off the ground. In short, the creature is not responsible for the whole of the story or for all the consequences of her action. Rather, she is responsible for playing well the role allotted her. C. S. Lewis has put the point well by appealing to another story, *King Lear*. In that play there is a character so insignificant that Shakespeare has not even given him a name; he is simply the "First Servant."

> All the characters around him—Regan, Cornwall, and Edmund—have fine long-term plans. They think they know how the story is going to end, and they are quite wrong. The servant has no such delusions. He has no notion how the play is going to go. But he understands the present scene. He sees an abomination (the blinding of old Gloucester) taking place. He will not stand it. His sword is out and pointed at his master's breast in a moment: then Regan stabs him dead from behind.

And what shall we say of such a role, how evaluate such a life? Lewis concludes: "This is his whole part: eight lines all told. But if it were real life and not a play, that is the part it would be best to have acted."[7]

We may say that Foot's position, like the traditional Catholic view, is an anti-consequentialist ethic, and such an ethic is grounded in the Christian story. Our duty as creatures is not necessarily to achieve the best consequences in general, but to act out with fidelity the responsibilities given us. To say that certain deeds ought not to be done even in order to achieve what seem to be the best consequences on the whole is to say that the creature is responsible for doing all the good he morally can, not all that he can. To understand ourselves as creatures is to believe that we ought not to step out of the story and think of ourselves as author rather than character. We are not to orchestrate the final denouement; we are simply to be responsible.

It is a measure of how much this Christian story has lost its hold on our consciousness that many today may be horror-stricken by any counsel that we think of our responsibility in terms that limit it. But, of course, as anyone who knows the Christian story can attest, this is not an attempt to evade guilt; rather, it is an attempt to understand ourselves as what we are: creatures, not the creator; characters, not the author. It may be that we cannot understand ourselves this way (and limit our action accordingly) apart from faith that the Author of the story knows what he is doing and can bring it to a successful completion. Within the terms of the story, a situation that seems to invite us to give greater weight to a positive than a negative duty is to be viewed as a *temptation*—an inducement once again to view ourselves as gods and to try to take into our own hands the plot of the story and unlimited responsibility for the consequences of our action.

That kind of unlimited responsibility ought to be accepted by no one except God. Perhaps, or course, the story will turn out all wrong and the consequences will be deplorable. That is the risk we take as we live in hope. Within the confines of the story, however, that possibility must be understood, not as a call to moral agents to take over the Creator's responsibility, but as a temptation to believe that God either cannot bring off what he has said he can do or does not want to. It raises, in short, either the old problem of evil or a straightforward temptation for faith. In either case, our first recourse ought not to be to revise our judgment about what moral agents, understood as creatures, can rightfully do. There is good theological reason to support Foot's distinction between negative and positive duties as well as her belief that, in a conflict between the two, negative duties take priority. This should, in fact, be part of what it means to call ourselves creatures.

Thus far I have simply tried to make clear why human lives not in conflict should be protected from direct attack, even if the cost of doing so is the sacrifice of other goods. But what of cases where life conflicts with equal life? Despite the progress of medical science, circumstances still arise in which a woman will die without an abortion. There are also instances (for example, some cases of chronic heart or kidney disease, in which pregnancy greatly increases the strain on heart or kidneys) when the woman's life is in greater danger, even if not immediately threatened, if no abortion is performed. This brings us to the second element in the traditional Catholic position, to the related concepts of indirect killing and double effect. How, granting what has been said above, could abortion be justified even in such conflict cases? After all, if one life conflicts with another, both are still human lives. Each is still our "neighbor"—one whose very presence among us calls out for respect and protection. It is, therefore, morally perplexing to encounter a case in which serving one neighbor seems to require turning against the well-being of the other. But this seems to be the structure of a genuine conflict situation: We must either (a) serve neither neighbor; or (b) turn against the well-being of one of the conflicting lives. It is, in other words, a situation in which *doing good* seems to entail *doing evil,* thus creating an incoherence in the fundamental moral law.

The example from Philippa Foot that I used above tends to overlook this fact for a very simple reason. The case of the runaway railroad engine (an analogue to a permitted killing case) is one in which the agent is already in action and can do nothing to avoid killing either one or five people. He cannot stop; nonintervention is not a possibility for him. But it is always a possibility in cases where the lives of fetus and mother come into conflict. It is always possible to "do nothing" and permit nature to take its course. It is common, therefore, to think in terms of three alternatives when facing such conflict cases: (1) We can abandon equal regard for human lives and intervene in order to preserve the life we consider of greater worth; (2) we can remain equalitarian (valuing both lives in conflict equally) and stand aside; (3) we can remain equalitarian but nevertheless intervene by reasoning in double-effect categories.[8] If, affirming the equal dignity of every human being made in God's image, we reject the first of these approaches, we are left with two options, each of which has played a role in traditional Catholic moral theology.

In conflict cases, Catholic thought has sought a way to do good (intervene) while at the same time avoiding evil (refraining from directly attacking innocent life). The solution offered has been that of "indirect killing." A standard example will make it clear: Catholic moralists have permitted abortion for a pregnant woman with a cancerous uterus. Removal of the cancerous uterus is the direct intention, the target, of the intervention. The death of the fetus, though foreseen and permitted, is nevertheless not approved and not aimed at. Hence, in such an intervention, one act is carried out, but it is an act with a double effect (removing the cancerous uterus; killing the fetus). The evil effect is not intended; that is, not embraced as part of the agent's aim or plan. And it is possible to describe the intervention in such a way that the agent's plan of action (his intention) can be seen to be saving the life of the mother by a means that, as it happens, also involves indirectly taking the life of the fetus.

We can compare this to a slightly different case, alluded to by Paul Ramsey: that of a woman needing an induced abortion as a first step toward dealing with a case of misplaced, acute appendicitis (in which the pregnant woman's appendix will rupture if the fetus is not aborted so that the physicians can get to the appendix).[9] Intervention here would *not* fit the paradigm of indirect killing. For here two distinct acts are involved, the first of which kills the fetus and is a means toward the second, which deals with the threat to the mother's life. In such a case it is difficult to claim that we have not embraced the death of the fetus within our aim— that we have not aimed at the evil effect in order to achieve the good effect. This is precisely what double-effect reasoning prohibits. An act may often have several effects, some good and others evil. That alone does not mean it may not be done. The key is that, though the evil effects may well be foreseen and permitted to occur, the act must be such that we can sensibly and honestly say that we do not aim at them. Our intention and aim must be directed only at the good effects. If this is not a fair description of

the act, we are doing evil that good may come of it—or, to change
the terminology, violating a negative duty for the sake of a positive duty. In the case of the cancerous uterus, intervention would
be permitted and the killing indirect (only the good effect, not the
evil effect, would be aimed at). In the case of the misplaced, acute
appendicitis, we would, it appears, have to stand aside and do
nothing in order to value the conflicted lives equally. And almost
certainly in those cases where the threat to the mother's life is real
but less immediate (e.g., if she suffers from severe kidney disease),
double-effect reasoning would not justify intervention. For an
intervention could hardly be said to aim at any organ in the
woman's body (in the way one could aim at the cancerous uterus);
it would have to target the fetus.

This comparison of cases points to the difficulties a Protestant is
likely to feel with the attempt to reason morally about abortion
using only the concepts of indirect killing and double effect. They
are useful, indeed, necessary concepts in moral reasoning. But here
they are not sufficient. If we try to permit intervention in all conflict
cases, we will have to stretch the notion of indirect killing beyond
recognition. If, on the other hand, we adhere to a straightforward
notion of what double effect permits, we will be left with nonintervention as our only course of action in some cases. What we need is
a perspective that will permit us to intervene in all (not just some)
conflict cases but that will countenance abortion only in such cases.

An Alternative View

We noted above the three possibilities that seem to be available
when we confront a conflict of life with equal life: (1) Let one life
count for more than the other; (2) value both lives equally, stand

aside, and let nature do as it will; (3) intervene in those cases where the killing can be justified as indirect. Having rejected the first of these, we considered how both (2) and (3) enter into the traditional Catholic position on abortion. But there is a fourth possibility, a somewhat different sort of justification put forward by Helmut Thielicke. In conflict cases, he notes, we come face to face with the disorder sin brings to nature, not with an unblemished creation reflecting perfectly the will of its Creator. And he further suggests that in such cases "we grant to medical assistance the mission to set forth in a signlike (though admittedly imperfect) way God's *real* will for the world and allow it to be a reminder of the original perfect creation and a promise of the world to come."[10] That is, we are to give expression to our belief (and hope) that the heavenly Father is a loving, not an indifferent, Father—one who does not hesitate to involve himself in our disordered world.

We might put Thielicke's point this way: In a conflict case we must either serve neither neighbor or turn directly against the well-being of one neighbor. But to serve neither neighbor is *inhuman* in a specifiable sense. Human bonds can reach their fruition only when characterized by love—that is, by some measure of giving and receiving. It is our task to shape "natural" events in such a way that they *are* humanized—are characterized by giving and receiving to the degree they can be. To require nonintervention makes it impossible so to humanize a case where life conflicts with equal life. (Obviously, it would be very different should the mother freely offer herself on behalf of the child. In that instance the bond would be clearly and dramatically characterized by the giving and receiving that is love.) The requirement of nonintervention in parity conflict cases involves, therefore, an indifference to our human condition, a willingness to accept a bond that has not yet risen to the personal, human level. If we see this, we can also understand why abortion ought to be permitted in cases of pregnancy resulting from rape, even though these are not conflict cases in any normal sense. The fetus embodies the attack on the woman's person. To capture the moral reality of this situation we might borrow language from the ethics of warfare and describe the fetus as an unjust aggressor on the woman's life—not formally, of course, as if this were the fetus's aim, but materially, since it is in fact the case. Here again, the woman whose personhood has been violated might choose to wrest some human significance from her tragedy by carrying the child to term and bearing the burden that involves. But to require her to do so would once again make it impossible for giving and receiving actually to transform the situation.

This justification of intervention in parity conflict cases eschews the concept of indirect killing, but it does not cease to affirm the equal worth of fetus and mother. Only *after* Thielicke has justified intervention—as a means of witnessing in signlike way to the real will of God, or, we might say, a means of humanizing a natural event—does he discuss the possibly permissible balancing of fetal against maternal life. That weighing is not involved in the justification of the intervention itself. Having seen that intervention is needed and justified, we may then grant the mother's claims a certain preeminence because, in truth, the child is living off her and is entirely dependent on her.

We have now the outlines of an alternative view. It would, like Catholic moral theology, limit intervention to cases where life conflicts with equal life (though perhaps construing that range of cases a little more broadly). This would be done by means of the distinction betweeen positive and negative duties, grounded in a recognition of our creaturely condition, and anchored thereby in the first article of the Christian creed. It would, unlike the traditional Catholic view, permit intervention in *all* parity conflict cases, recognizing the need to interject as least some element of giving and receiving into nature's tragedies in order to bear witness to God's own love. It would also permit intervention in cases of pregnancy resulting from forcible intercourse, on the grounds that the continued presence of the fetus incarnates the inhuman violation, not just of the woman's body, but of her person; that it is not inaccurate in this instance to picture the fetus as, materially, an unjust aggressor; and that, as in more ordinary conflict cases, we cannot rest content in acknowledging a situation entirely devoid of human acts of giving and receiving.

One problem remains. Earlier I characterized the core of the traditional Catholic view as involving two essential elements: (1) an affirmation of the equal right of every human life to protection; and (2) justification of indirect killing in some (but not all) cases where life conflicts with equal life. Much of this position's strength lies in its coherence. The interventions countenanced in (2) are permitted in a way that does not call into question premise (1), on which the position was founded. Direct killing is always proscribed, in accord with (1). The killings permitted under (2) are only those that can be understood to be indirect. Whatever the difficulties of this position, it achieves considerable coherence—no small virtue.

Can the same be said of the alternative I offer? If intervention is permitted in order to bear witness in a disordered world to the Creator's real will for the creation, what is there to prohibit us— on occasions other than actual cases of parity conflict between lives—from violating negative duties in order "to set forth in a signlike (though admittedly imperfect) way God's *real* will for the world"? Have we, in other words, justified intervention in terms that might permit it also in other cases that, though they manifest the disorder of a sinful world, are not themselves instances where life conflicts with equal life or situations in which there remains no other way to be humanly present in acts of giving and receiving? After all, there will be many circumstances that, though they do not so dramatically manifest the disorder of a sinful world and are not totally devoid of possibilities for giving and receiving, are nevertheless far from exemplifying God's real will for the world. Would it be permissible to violate negative duties in order to improve such situations? If it were permissible, the two halves of my suggested position—limiting intervention to conflict cases *only;* justifying it in *all* such cases—would prove incoherent. We would be forced back to a choice between nonintervention and simply weighing magnitudes of evil.

It may help us to appreciate what is at stake theologically if we step back for a moment from the problem of abortion and consider a different problem in medical ethics. In his seminal work, *The Patient as Person,*[11] Paul Ramsey has a chapter in which he discusses ethical considerations involved in the self-giving of vital organs. The bulk of the chapter, which cannot be adequately summarized here, examines Catholic and Protestant justifications for such self-giving. Catholic justifications, all versions of a principle of totality, rely on some benefit believed to accrue to the donor. Any such justification of organ donation will, of course, have to be a principle of totality that takes into account the spiritual and moral well-being of the donor. The donor is permitted to sacrifice an organ and injure his physical well-being for the sake of his total personal welfare—the fulfillment that this act of giving will bring him.

On the other hand, "a possible justification of organ transplantation from living donors that might be developed within the ambit of Protestant ethics would rest the matter upon charitable consent alone; the benefit aimed at would be the benefit to the recipient, not the donor's own higher wholeness."[12] Thus, Ramsey seeks to justify organ donation by appeal to the self-giving spirit of Christian love. Having done this, however, he immediately confronts a problem. To stress love alone lends tremendous pressure to appeals for medical intervention to help someone in need. Such a justification of self-giving may, Ramsey writes, "precisely because of its freedom from the moorings of self-concern, be likely to fly too high above concern for the bodily integrity of the donor."[13] At this point, he suggests, physicians will have to "save us from the moralists" and remain the "only Hebrews." Though stated metaphorically, Ramsey's point is that it will never be sufficient to speak only of love. Such talk, in isolation, will be unable to limit pressures for intervention (pressures to "do good"); indeed, it will intensify such pressures. Rather, we must make it clear that ours is always to be a *creaturely* love. There is a fine line—but a crucial one—that separates genuine creaturely love from a love that soars too high and forgets its created dependence. And a love that does soar too high, in thus forgetting its creaturely moorings, has, in fact, become sin. Indeed, it has been subtly transmuted into that primal sin: pride. So fine is the line that divides creaturely love from a renewed attempt to be "like God."

Something similar happens when we try to construct a moral standpoint on abortion. We find ourselves pulled in two directions. On the one hand, when we consider the limits our creaturely condition places upon us, we are driven to prohibit intervention. For, after all, the good we are to do is only the good that can morally be done. We do not author the whole story. When, on the other hand, we take seriously the call to let our life be shaped by the self-giving love of Christ, the pressures to intervene—to testify to a God who is loving, not indifferent—become intense. An incoherence seems driven into the very heart of our position.

This helps us to see what is at stake theologically and shows why such incoherence must be risked and both halves of the position maintained. We would be mistaken—theologically mistaken—to choose either (a) nonintervention, or (b) simply weighing the costs and benefits involved in intervening. Neither would do justice to the full character of human relationships. The former divests such bonds of the giving and receiving necessary to humanize them. The latter ignores the limits of our creaturely responsibility. We need to do justice to both creation *and* redemption; both parts of the story God is telling must shape our action. If we cannot bring about a perfectly coherent fit between the two, that is perhaps not surprising. It is almost what we should expect of people whose status is that of pilgrims—people who find themselves in the middle of the story, often unable to discern its direction of movement, its total significance, or how the Author will manage to weave the many threads of the plot together in such a way as to resolve seeming incoherence.

We have theological reason, therefore, not to let ourselves be overcome by a desire for "foolish consistency." We need to justify intervention in parity conflict cases lest our witness seem to be to an indifferent rather than a loving Father. In conflict cases there is no other way to bear witness to God's real will for his creation, no other way to infuse some element of giving and receiving into the natural event. At the same time, there are good reasons for limiting intervention to just such cases. As sinful creatures we are always tempted to soar too high, to try to be as God, and to take final responsibility for the whole of the story. It is important that we limit our interventions in such a way that we remain human and creaturely.

Part Three
The End of Life

7

Euthanasia and Christian Vision

Every teacher has probably experienced, along with countless frustrations, moments in the classroom when something was said with perfect lucidity. I still recall one such moment some years ago when I was teaching a seminar dealing with ethical issues in death and dying. Knowing how difficult it can be to get students to consider these problems from within religious perspectives, I decided to force the issue at the outset by assigning as the first reading parts of those magnificent sections from Volume III/4 of Karl Barth's *Church Dogmatics* in which he discusses "Respect for Life" and "The Protection of Life." I gave the students little warning in advance, preferring to let the vigor and bombast of Barth's style have whatever effect it might.

The students, I must say in retrospect, probably thought more kindly of Barth (who had, after all, only written these sections) than of their teacher (who had assigned them to be read). But they good-naturedly went about doing the assignment, and our seminar had a worthwhile discussion—with students criticizing Barth and even sometimes defending him. Neither criticism nor defense was really my goal, however. It was understanding—understanding of death and dying within a perspective steeped in centuries of Christian life and thought—that I was seeking. And at one moment, even in a moment of criticism, we achieved that understanding.

One young woman in the class, seeking to explain why Barth puzzled her so, put it quite simply: "What I really don't like about

him is that he seems to think our lives are not our own." To
which, after a moment of awed silence, I could only respond: "If
you begin to see that about Barth, even if it gets under your skin
and offends you deeply, then indeed you have begun to understand what he is saying."

In his discussion of "The Protection of Life," and, in fact, within
his specific discussion of euthanasia, Barth notes many of the difficult questions we might raise that seem to nudge us in the direction
of approving euthanasia in certain tormenting cases. And then,
rejecting these "tempting questions," he responds with his own
typical flair: "All honour to the well-meaning humanitarianism of
underlying motive! But the derivation is obviously from another
book than that which we have thus far consulted."[1] In this chapter I
want to think about euthanasia not from the perspective of any
"well-meaning humanitarianism" but from within the perimeters
of Christian belief—though, as we will see, one of the most important things to note is that, within those boundaries, only what is
consonant with Christian belief can be truly humane.[2]

The Paradigm Case

Determining what really qualifies as euthanasia is no easy matter.
Need the person "euthanatized" be suffering terribly? Or, at least,
be near death? Suppose the person simply feels life is no longer
worth living in a particular condition that may be deeply dissatisfying, though not filled with suffering? Suppose the person's life is
filled with suffering or seemingly devoid of meaning but he is
unable to request euthanasia (because of a comatose condition,
senility, etc.)? Or suppose the person is suffering greatly but steadfastly says he does not want to die? Suppose the "euthanatizer's"
motive is not mercy but despair at the continued burden of caring
for the person—will that qualify?

The list of questions needing clarification is endless once we start down this path. But I intend to get off the path at once by taking as our focus a paradigm case of what must surely count as euthanasia. If we can understand why *this* is morally wrong, much else will fall into place. James Rachels has suggested that "the clearest possible case of euthanasia" would be one having the following five features:[3]

(1) The person is deliberately killed.
(2) The person would have died soon anyway.
(3) The person was suffering terrible pain.
(4) The person asked to be killed.
(5) The motive for the killing was mercy—to provide the person with as good a death as possible under the circumstances.

Such a case is not simply "assisted suicide," since the case requires the presence of great suffering, the imminence of death in any case, and a motive of mercy. Furthermore, considering this sort of case sets aside arguments about nonvoluntary and involuntary euthanasia and gives focus to our discussion.[4] If this case of voluntary euthanasia is permissible, other cases may also be (or may not). If this case is morally wrong, we are less likely to be able to argue for euthanasia in nonvoluntary and involuntary circumstances.

Aim and Result

One way of arguing that the paradigm case of euthanasia is morally permissible (perhaps even obligatory) is to claim that it does not differ in morally relevant ways from other acts that most of us approve. Consider a patient whose death is imminent, who is suffering terribly, and who may suddenly stop breathing and require resuscitation. We may think it best not to resuscitate such a person but simply to let him die. What could be the morally significant difference between such a "letting die" and simply giving this person a lethal injection that would end his life (and suffering) just as quickly? If it is morally right not to prolong his dying when he ceases breathing for a few moments, why is it morally wrong to kill him quickly and painlessly? Each act responds to the fact that death is imminent and recognizes that terrible suffering calls for relief. And the result in each case is the same: death.

In order to appreciate the important difference between these possibilities, we must distinguish what we *aim* at in our action from the *result* of the action. Or, to paraphrase Charles Fried, we must distinguish between those actions that we invest with the personal involvement of purpose and those that merely "run through" our person.[5] This is a distinction that moral reflection can scarcely get along without. For example, if we fail to distinguish between aim and result, we will be unable to see any difference between the self-sacrifice of a martyr and the suicide of a person weary of life. The result is the same for each: death. But the aim or purpose is quite different. Whereas the suicide aims at his death, the martyr aims at faithfulness to God (or loyalty of some other sort). Both martyr and suicide recognize in advance that the result of their choice and act will be death. But the martyr does not aim at death.

This distinction between aim and result is also helpful in explaining the moral difference between euthanatizing a suffering person near death and simply letting such a person die. Suppose this patient were to stop breathing, we were to reject the possibility of resuscitation, and then the person were suddenly to begin breathing again. Would we, simply because we had been willing to let this patient die, now proceed to smother him so that he would indeed die? Hardly. And the fact that we would not indicates that we did not *aim* at his death (in rejecting resuscitation), though his death could have been one *result* of what we did aim at (namely, proper care for him in his dying). By contrast, if we euthanatized such a person by giving him a lethal injection, we would indeed aim at his death; we would invest the act of aiming at his death with the personal involvement of our purpose.

A rejoinder: It is possible to grant the distinction between aim and result while still claiming that euthanasia in our paradigm case would be permissible (or obligatory). It may be true that there is a difference between allowing a patient to die and aiming at someone's death. But if the suffering of the dying person is truly intense and the person requests death, on what grounds could we refuse to assist him? If we refuse on the grounds that it would be wrong for us to aim at his death (which will certainly come soon anyway, after still more terrible suffering), are we not saying that we are unwilling to do him a great good if doing it requires that we dirty our hands in any way? To put the matter this way makes it seem that our real concern is with our own moral rectitude, not with the needs of the sufferer. It seems that we are so concerned about ourselves that in our eagerness to narrow the scope of our moral responsibility we have lost sight of the need and imperative to offer care.

This is, it should be obvious, what ethicists call a *consequentialist* rejoinder. It suggests that the good results (relieving the suffering) are sufficiently weighty to make the aim (of killing) morally permissible or obligatory. And, as far as I can tell, this rejoinder has become increasingly persuasive to large numbers of people.

Consequentialism may be described as that moral theory which holds that from the fact that some state of affairs *ought to be* it follows that we *ought to do* whatever is necessary and possible to bring about that state of affairs. And, although teleological theories of morality are very ancient, consequentialism as a full-blown moral theory is modern, traceable largely to Bentham and Mill in the late eighteenth and early nineteenth centuries. To remember this is instructive, since it is not implausible to suggest that such a moral theory would be most persuasive when Christendom had, in large measure, ceased to be Christian. Those who know themselves as creatures—not Creator—will recognize limits even upon their obligation to do good. As creatures we are to do all the good we can, but this means all the good we "morally can"—all the good we can within certain limits. It may be that the Creator *ought to do* whatever is necessary to bring about states of affairs that *ought to be,* but we stand under no such godlike imperative.[6]

One of the best ways to understand the remarkable appeal today of consequentialism as a moral theory is to see it as an ethic for those who (a) remain morally serious, but (b) have ceased to believe in a God whose providential care will ultimately bring about whatever ought to be the case. If God is not there to accomplish what ought to be, we are the most likely candidates to shoulder the burden of that responsibility.[7] Conversely, it may be that we can make sense of distinguishing between two acts whose *result* is the same but whose *aim* is different only if we believe that our responsibilities as creatures are limited—that the responsibility for achieving certain results has been taken out of our hands (or, better, never given us in the first place). It ought to be the case that dying people not suffer terribly. But, at least for the Christian, it does not follow from that "ought to be" that we "ought to do" whatever is necessary—even euthanasia—to relieve them of that suffering.[8]

We are now in a position to see something important about the argument that claims euthanasia (in the paradigm case) is permissible because it does not differ morally from the cases of "letting die" that most of us approve. This argument often begins in a failure to distinguish aim and result; however, it is, as we have seen, difficult for moral theory to get along without this distinction. Seeing this, we recognize that the argument really becomes a claim that if the results are sufficiently good any aim necessary to achieve them is permissible. And precisely at this turn in the argument it may be difficult to keep "religion" and "morality" in those neat and separate compartments we have fashioned for them. At this point one steeped in Christian thought and committed to Christian life may wish to say with Barth: All honor to the well-meaning humanitarianism—and it is well-meaning. But the derivation—fit only for those who would, even if reluctantly, be "like God"—is obviously "derived from another book" than that which Christians are wont to consult.

Aim and Motive

If the distinction between aim and result makes it difficult to justify euthanasia in the paradigm case, another distinction may be more useful. We might suggest that the act of euthanatizing be redescribed in terms of the motive of mercy. We could describe the act not as killing but as relieving suffering. Or, rather than engaging in such wholesale redescription of the act, we might simply argue that our moral evaluation of the act cannot depend solely on its *aim* but must also consider its *motive*.

Consider the following illustration.[9] A condemned prisoner is in his cell only minutes before his scheduled execution. As he sits in fear and anguish, certain of his doom, another man (who has managed to sneak into the prison) shoots and kills him. This man is either (a) the father of children murdered by the prisoner, or (b) a close friend of the prisoner. In case (a) he shoots because he will not be satisfied simply to have the man executed. He desires that his own hand should bring about the prisoner's death. In case (b) the friend shoots because he wishes to spare his friend the terror and anguish of those last minutes, to deliver him from the indignity of the sheer animal fright he is undergoing.

Would it be proper to describe the father's act in (a) as an act of killing and the friend's in (b) as an act of relieving suffering? Although many people may be tempted to do so, it muddies rather than clarifies our analysis. If anything is clear in these cases, it is that both the vengeful father and the compassionate friend *aim* to kill, though their *motives* are very different. Only by refusing to redescribe the aim of the act in terms of its motive do we keep the moral issue clearly before us. That issue is whether our moral evaluation of the act should depend solely on the agent's *aim* or whether that evaluation must also include the *motive*.

That the motive makes *some* difference almost everyone would agree. Few of us would be content to analyze the two cases simply as instances of "aiming to kill" without considering the quite different motives. The important question, however, is whether the praiseworthy motive of relieving suffering should so dominate our moral reflection that it leads us to term the act "right." I want to suggest that it should not, at least not within the boundaries of Christian belief.

One might think that Christian emphasis on the overriding importance of love as a motive would suggest that whatever was done out of love was right. And, to be sure, Christians often talk this way. Such talk, however, must be done against the background assumptions of Christian anthropology. Apart from that background of meaning we may doubt whether we have really understood the motive of love correctly. We need, therefore, to sketch in the background against which we can properly understand what loving care for a suffering person should be.

Barth writes that human life "must always be regarded as a divine act of trust."[10] This means that all human life is "surrounded by a particular solemnity," which, if recognized, will lead us to "treat it with respect." At the same time, however, "life is no second God, and therefore the respect due to it cannot rival the reverence owed to God." One who knows this will seek to live life "within its appointed limits." Recognizing our life as a trust, we will be moved not by an "absolute will to live" but a will to live within these limits. Hence, when we understand ourselves as creatures, we will both value God's gift of life and recognize that the Giver himself constitutes the limit beyond which we ought not to value the gift. "Temporal life is certainly not the highest of all goods. Just because it belongs to God, man may be forbidden to will its continuation at all costs." And at the same time, "if life is not the highest possession, then it is at least the highest and all-inclusive price" that human beings can pay. In short, life is a great good, but not the greatest good (which is fidelity to God).

Death, the final enemy of life, must also be understood dialectically. The human mind can take, and has quite naturally taken, two equally plausible attitudes toward death.[11] We can regard death as of no consequence, heeding the Epicurean maxim that while we are alive death is not yet here, and when death is here we are no more. Thus the human being, in a majestic transcendence of the limits of earthly life, might seek to soar beyond the limits of finitude and find his good elsewhere. If death is of no consequence, we may seek it in exchange for some important good. Equally natural to the human mind is a seemingly opposite view—that death is the *summum malum,* the greatest evil, to be avoided at all costs. Such a view, finding good only in earthly life, can find none in suffering and death.

The Christian mind, however, transcending what is "natural" and correcting it in light of the book it is accustomed to consult, has refused to take either of these quite plausible directions. Understood within the biblical narrative, death is an ambivalent phenomenon—too ambivalent to be seen only as the greatest of all evils, or as indifferent. Since the world narrated by the Bible begins in God and moves toward God, earthly life is his trust, to be sustained faithfully, and his gift, to be valued and cared for. When life is seen from this perspective, we cannot say that death and suffering are of no consequence; on the contrary, we can even say with Barth that the human task in the face of suffering and death is not to accept but to offer "final resistance."[12] It is just as true, though, that death could never be the greatest evil. That title must be reserved for disobedience to and disbelief in God—a refusal to live within our appointed limits. So we can also repeat with Barth that "life is no second God."[13] We remember, after all, that Jesus goes to the cross in the name of obedience to his Father. We need not glorify or seek suffering, but we must be struck by the fact that a human being who is a willing sufferer stands squarely in the center of Christian piety. Jesus bears his suffering not because it is desirable but because the Father allots it to him within the limits of his earthly life. Death is—there is no way to put the matter simply—a great evil that God can turn to his good purposes. It is an evil that must ordinarily be resisted but that must also at some point be acknowledged. We can and should acknowledge what we do not and should not seek. George Orwell, himself an "outsider," nicely summarized these background assumptions of Christian anthropology:

> The Christian attitude towards death is not that it is something to be welcomed, or that it is something to be met with stoical indifference, or that it is something to be avoided as long as possible; but that it is something profoundly tragic which has to be gone through with. A Christian, I suppose, if he were offered the chance of everlasting life on this earth would refuse it, but he would still feel that death is profoundly sad.[14]

This vision of the world, and of the meaning of life and death, has within Christendom given guidance to those reflecting on human suffering and dying. That moral guidance has amounted to the twofold proposition that, though we might properly cease to oppose death while aiming at other choice-worthy goods in life (hence, the possibility of martyrdom), we ought never to aim at death as either our end or our means.

Against this background of belief we can better understand what *love* and *care* must be within a world construed in Christian terms. In *this* world no action that deliberately hastens death can be called "loving." Not because the euthanatizer need have any evil motive. Indeed, as the case of the compassionate friend makes clear, the one who hastens death may seem to have a praiseworthy motive. Rather, such action cannot be loving because it cannot be part of the meaning of commitment to the well-being of another human being within the appointed limits of earthly life. The benevolence of the euthanatizer is enough like love to give us pause, to tempt us to call it love. And *perhaps* it may even be the closest those who feel themselves to bear full responsibility for relief of suffering and production of good in our world can come to love. But it is not the creaturely love that Christians praise, a love that can sometimes do no more than suffer as best we can with the sufferer.

Christian Love Enacted and Inculcated

Against this background—a background that pours meaning into words like "love" and "care"—we can contemplate the kind of case often considered in discussions of euthanasia.[15] A person may be in severe pain, certain to die within only a few days. Most of us would agree that further "lifesaving" treatments were not in order for such a person, that they would do no more than prolong his dying. Why, one may ask, do we decline to subject such a patient to useless treatments? Because, the answer goes, he is in agony and it would be wrong to prolong that agony needlessly. But then, if we face the facts honestly, we must admit that it takes this patient longer to die—and prolongs his suffering—if we simply withhold treatment than if we euthanatize him. Hence, there seems to be a contradiction within our reasoning. The motive for withholding treatment was a humanitarian one: relief of suffering. But in refusing to take the next step and euthanatize the patient, we prolong his suffering and thereby belie our original motive. Hence, the conclusion follows, quite contrary to the moral guidance embedded in the Christian vision of the world: Either we should keep this person alive as long as possible (and not pretend that our motive is relief of suffering), or we should be willing to euthanatize him.

The argument gets much of its force from the seeming simplicity of the dilemma, but that simplicity is misleading. For, at least for Christian vision, the fundamental imperative is not "minimize suffering" but "maximize love and care." In that Christian world, in which death and suffering are great evils but not the greatest evil, love can never include in its meaning hastening a fellow human being toward (the evil of) death, nor can it mean a refusal to acknowledge death when it comes (as an evil, but not the greatest evil). We can only know what the imperative "maximize love" means if we understand it against the background assumptions that make intelligible for Christians words like "love" and "care." The Christian mind has certainly not recommended that we seek suffering or call it an unqualified good, but it is an evil that, when endured faithfully, can be redemptive. William May has noted how parents in our time think that love for their children means, above all else, protecting those children from suffering. "As conscientious parents, they operate as though the powers that are decisive in the universe could not possibly do anything in and through the suffering of their children. . . . They take upon themselves the responsibilities of a savior-figure. . . ."[16] May sees clearly that "minimize suffering" and "maximize love" are not identical imperatives and do not offer the same direction for human action. Perhaps the direction they give may often be the same, but at times—especially when we consider what it is proper to do for the irretrievably dying—we will discover how sharply they may differ.

I suggested above that we should not redescribe the *aim* of an act in terms of its *motive*. (We should not say that an act of killing a suffering person was simply an act of relieving suffering. We should say rather that we aimed at the death of a person in order to relieve his suffering. This keeps the moral issue more clearly before us.) But by now it will be evident that I have in fact gone some way toward redescribing the *motive* of the act in terms of its *aim*. (If the act is aimed at hastening the death of the suffering person, we should not see it as motivated by love.) Is this any better? The answer, I think, is "it depends."

It would not be better—it might even be worse—if my purpose were to deny any humanitarian motive to the person tempted to euthanatize a sufferer. Few people would find such a denial persuasive, and because we would not we are tempted to turn in the opposite direction and describe the act's aim in terms of its motive. We *do* recognize a difference between the vengeful father and the compassionate friend even though both aim to kill the condemned prisoner, and we want our moral judgments to be sufficiently nuanced to take account of these differences. The simple truth is that our evaluation of the act described in terms of aim and our evaluation of the act described in terms of motive often fall apart. In a world broken by sin and its consequences this should perhaps come as no surprise. Christians believe that we sinners—all of us—are not whole, and many of the stubborn problems of systematic ethical reflection testify to the truth of that belief. It is our lack of wholeness that is displayed in our inability to arrive at one judgment (or even one description) "whole and entire" of a single act. We find ourselves in a world in which people may sometimes seem to aim at doing evil from the best of motives (and think they must do so). And then we are tempted to elide aim and motive and call that evil at which they aim "good."

No amount of ethical reflection can heal this rift in our nature. From that predicament we will have to look for a deliverance greater than ethics can offer. Here and now, however, in our broken world, we do better to take the aim of an act as our guiding light in describing and evaluating the act—and then evaluate the motive in light of this aim. This is better because moral reflection is not primarily a tool for fixing guilt and responsibility (in which case motive would come to the fore). It is, first and foremost, one of the ways in which we train ourselves and others to see the world rightly. We would be wrong to assert that no euthanatizer has or can have humanitarian motive. But if we want not so much to fix praise or blame as to teach the meaning of the word "love," we are not wrong to say that love could never euthanatize. In the Christian world this is true. And in that world we know the right name for our own tendency to call those other, seemingly humanitarian, motives "love." The name for that tendency is *temptation*. We are being tempted to be "like God" when we toy with the possibility of defining our love—and the meaning of humanity—apart from the appointed limits of human life.

To redescribe the motive in terms of the act's aim, to attempt to *inculcate* a vision of the world in which love could never euthanatize, is therefore not only permissible but necessary for Christians. It is the only proper way to respond to the supposed dilemmas we are confronted with by reasoning that brackets Christian background assumptions from the outset. The Christian moral stance that emerges here is not a club with which to beat over the head those who disagree. It does not provide a superior vantage point from which to deny them any humanitarian motive in the ordinary sense. But it *is* a vision of what "humanity" and "humanitarian motives" should be. We may therefore say of those who disagree: "All honour to the well-meaning humanitarianism of underlying motive! But the derivation is obviously from another book than that which we have thus far consulted."

8

If This Baby Could Choose . . .

Many of the moral problems raised by the practice of medicine today require that decisions be made in cases where the patient cannot even participate in the decision-making process, much less actually make a decision. Some of the most difficult of such cases involve infants—e.g., whether to perform experiments that have potential for great benefit on infants who cannot give a free and informed consent, whether to carry out what were once called "extraordinary" treatments in order to preserve the lives of infants with defects that are life-threatening. I will focus on the second of these issues—care of defective newborns (a term that today includes conditions as diverse as Down's syndrome, spina bifida, and Tay-Sachs disease).

That we must reach decisions in such cases is clear, but no one is too certain how best to do it. Many of us believe that we ought to seek whatever is in the child's best interests. Some disagree. They hold that when the child's best interests conflict with the interests of its family or society, or when the child is comparatively devoid of potential for "meaningful" life, we should weigh other factors more heavily in determining and seeking a "greatest good." Here I will not argue—but will presume—that we ought to seek whatever is in the child's best interests. How to do this is, however, far from clear. Two approaches often used are: (1) to attempt to substitute our judgment for the child's (to ask what the child would choose if it could), and (2) to ask what any reasonable person would choose in similar circumstances.

The burden of my argument will be to suggest that—given what I think is a correct description of what takes place when competent patients make their own decisions in similar circumstances—it makes little sense to attempt to use either of these standards in deciding for incompetent patients such as newborns. The reasonable-person standard does not really arrive at a patient-centered decision, and the substituted-judgment standard (applied to the case of newborns) is incoherent—or so I will argue. The most attractive alternative to these standard views is Paul Ramsey's "medical indications" policy, which I will defend and then worry about. In order to delimit the scope of this discussion I will concentrate on the opposing positions of Ramsey and Richard McCormick.[1]

The Point at Issue

It is best to begin by eliminating considerations that, however important elsewhere, are not really at issue here. Both men are agreed that treatment ought not simply to prolong the dying of an incurably ill patient. Ramsey is now careful to say that a patient may be terminally ill and yet not be irretrievably dying (p. 187). But neither Ramsey nor McCormick would for a moment suggest that a patient whose life can be helped by no known treatment should receive anything other than the "treatment" now appropriate: care, comfort, and relief of pain in his dying.

There is also substantial agreement between McCormick and Ramsey with respect to the right of *competent* patients to refuse treatment. Rather than speaking of a right to refuse treatment, Ramsey prefers to emphasize that the patient is entitled to "free and informed participation in medical decisions affecting him" (p. 157), but there is no serious disagreement here. Similarly, Ramsey prefers—even in the case of competent patients—to speak only of treatments medically indicated or not indicated; however, in deciding whether a treatment is or is not indicated, he permits and encourages the participation of the competent patient. Indeed, he explicitly grants (though in a concessive clause!) that a competent patient may use quality-of-life considerations in deciding to refuse treatment (p. 155). McCormick holds that, although treatment refusal by a competent patient may not be "frivolous," the patient may still decide by weighing a wide variety of factors (all of which could never be specified in advance): the burden of treatment, the quality of life it is likely to offer, cost of the treatment in financial and psychological terms to family and friends (p. 36). There seems no reason to think Ramsey would disagree with the substance of that position, however inclined he might be to formulate it differently.

The point at issue turns, therefore, on what Ramsey calls the "voiceless, nondying patient"; that is, one who is neither irretrievably dying nor competent to make decisions about the future course of treatment. A Down's syndrome baby born with an intestinal obstruction and a spina bifida baby would both be examples of voiceless, nondying patients. Neither is competent to refuse treatment. But also, neither is dying. For the Down's syndrome baby, a relatively simple operation may be all that is needed; for the spina bifida baby, a continuing series of operations may be required.

Obviously, for patients like these a proxy decision regarding treatment must be made by parents or a guardian. How shall they do so, and what considerations should guide them? McCormick suggests that one must ask what, in the judgment of reasonable people, would be in the "best overall interests of the patient" (p. 36). He stresses that the mere fact of consensus by reasonable people is not itself the right-making characteristic. That is, I presume, because we might discover seemingly reasonable people reaching consensus on a policy we thought morally wrong. What he wants to ensure as much as possible, however, is that the best overall interests of the patient are considered. And *if* we presume that an infant would choose (if it could) the treatment in its best interests, and *if* in turn we determine what is in the infant's best interests by consulting reasonable people, we can, with some measure of confidence, say that the infant would choose this treatment if he or she could choose. Thus McCormick combines the "reasonable person" and "substituted judgment" standards, using the former to help him determine the latter.

The appeal to what reasonable people would think is made because—if we are asking what a patient would choose if he could, and if this patient, an infant, has no past history or "track record" of choices—it is difficult to know how else to proceed. McCormick summarizes his position as follows: "If the situation is such that most or very many of us would not want life-preserving treatment *in that condition,* it would be morally prudent (reasonable) to conclude that life-preserving treatment is not morally required for this particular person" (p. 36). But notice, there is nothing particularly patient-centered about asking, "Would a reasonable person want this treatment?" That question asks not what would be in the best overall interests of *this* patient but, instead, whether most or many of the rest of us would choose treatment were we in a similar condition. And the question takes on the appearance of patient-centeredness only when conjoined with the attempt to substitute our judgment for that of the infant. Therefore, it is the attempt to make this substitution that requires our attention.

Why Substituted Judgment Won't Work

McCormick himself admits that it is "all but impossible" for us to "extrapolate backwards on what kind of life will be acceptable to the infant" (p. 36). Rather than eschewing the attempt, however, he decides that we must try to do the "all but impossible." We can begin to understand the incoherence of this suggestion if we consider the nature of decisions made by competent patients.

The competent patient may—Ramsey and McCormick are agreed—consider a variety of factors in deciding whether to refuse or consent to treatment. He may consider the value (to himself) of continued existence, his personal aspirations not yet realized, the burden and expense of the proposed treatment, his responsibilities to others, the degree of relief the treatment promises—in short, countless factors, none of them "frivolous." In my view, however, we would be mistaken to imagine that the competent patient is weighing the relative value of these competing factors, for they are incommensurable, and the scale on which they could be weighed or the lowest common denominator to which they could be reduced does not exist. Morality here is not a matter of scientific measurement, and moral reflection is not a matter of technique. When, therefore, the competent patient considers the various—incommensurable and incompatible—goods involved, she is not arriving at a *discovery* about some single right choice to make in these circumstances. There is no such right answer, no choice that someone else in the same circumstances would be "unreasonable" to veto.

Instead of making a discovery, the competent patient makes a *decision*. She decides how she will live—or how to live while dying. She chooses certain goods at the expense of other goods and, in so doing, shapes her own existence and character to some degree. If we insist on using language of "discovery" and "weighing" in such contexts, we must be clear about what it can mean. The relative weight of the conflicting goods is known—and known *only* for the person deciding—*after* the decision has been made. For another patient similarly situated the relative weight of the goods may be different and will likewise be known only after the fact of decision. The only "discovery" we make in such circumstances is a discovery of something about ourselves, the kind of people we will be because we have chosen to be.[2]

If this account of decisions by competent patients is correct, we can see that it is incoherent—not just "all but impossible"—to "extrapolate backwards on what kind of life will be acceptable to the infant." Were competent patients in such circumstances weighing commensurable goods in order to discover some general truth, the discoveries they made about the relative claims of these goods would be applicable to decisions about incompetent patients in analogous circumstances. But since competent patients are not doing this, since they are freely determining the person they will be and the life they will live, it makes little sense to suggest that we can or should try to do this for the infant. Someone else's *discovery* about how certain goods should be balanced might be applicable to infants in similar circumstances; someone else's *decision* to be a self of a particular sort can have no such applicability.

The Turn to Medical Indications

It seems, therefore, that McCormick's attempt to use "reasonableness" to get at the infant's best interests is a dead end as long as these "best interests" are couched in the subjective terms of what the infant would choose if it could. Ramsey offers a different approach. He attempts to bypass questions about what an infant would choose if it could by offering a more objective criterion. We should, he suggests, simply ask whether any available treatment will benefit the life the patient has. If a treatment offers benefit, it is medically indicated. The strength of this position lies in the fact that it clearly recognizes the differences between the situations of competent and incompetent patients. It does not attempt to blur the line between the two by suggesting that competent patients have discovered something that we can now apply to infants on the presumption that they too would be reasonable and make the same discovery. Competent patients *decide;* infants cannot. Competent patients determine *their* being, but no one else's. We are therefore forced to consider the best interests of infants in strictly medical terms: What, if anything, can we do that will benefit the lives they have?

This is, beyond any doubt, a powerful alternative. It attempts to be genuinely patient-centered and avoids the conceptual bog of substituted judgment. It gives rise, however, to a troublesome problem. It seems to leave us in the unhappy position of making *imperative* for infants treatments that many competent patients would decline for themselves—accepting for *all* infants what only *some* or, perhaps, *few* of the rest of us might accept for ourselves.[3]

In one sense this is simply the price we pay for recognizing the different situations of competent and incompetent patients. Yet, McCormick senses something puzzling about such an upshot, and perhaps he is right. McCormick had recognized that one of the reasons a proxy might decline treatment on behalf of an infant would be the "continuing burden" that the treatment would constitute for the child (p. 36). And that in itself is a purely patient-centered reason for declining treatment. But Ramsey's restriction of proxy consideration to the "indicated/not indicated" criterion tends to lose sight of this possibility. Thus, he can write with respect to treating a newborn with spina bifida: "I do not think that a series of ordinary treatments—closing the open spine, antibiotics, a contraption to deal with urinary incontinence, and a shunt to prevent hydrocephalus—today adds up to extraordinary medical care, except perhaps in the case of a conscious, competent patient who is able himself to refuse treatment" (p. 193). Here we see that Ramsey's criterion can too easily become what the ordinary/extraordinary distinction often was: a standard for what is customary and/or easily managed by physicians today. To let it become that, however, is to lose sight of the humane wisdom that recognizes that we might properly refuse treatment for an infant simply on the grounds of that treatment's "continuing burden" for the infant. No doubt this would not apply to a single operation on a Down's syndrome baby. But it seems possible that the kind and amount of treatment required for some spina bifida babies constitute a burden so severe (for the child) that one might in good conscience refuse such treatment on behalf of one's child.

I argued above that in treatment refusals by competent patients we cannot weigh costs and benefits, for the goods at stake are incommensurable. To say that, however, is not to say that we must always choose the benefits. Sometimes, at least, we may choose against—reject—the costs. If all the days and years of the child are equidistant from eternity and therefore of equal worth, we need not purchase some future days and years at any price.

McCormick would probably suggest that, like it or not, I am really making a covert judgment about what a reasonable weighing of costs and benefits would involve, and I have deliberately used language that elicits such a response. But I think it a mistaken response. I am trying to take with full seriousness the fact that in difficult cases of treatment refusal no such weighing is possible—and none, in fact, takes place. In most cases, therefore, it makes good sense to say with Ramsey that the only way to serve the best interests of the child is to do whatever can be done to benefit the life it has. This is, of course, to construe "best interests" more narrowly than we would, as competent patients, in making our own decision. But that is just the point. Until such time as a child can itself make these decisions, it does not have "best interests" in the broader sense that the rest of us do, for that broader sense involves decision. At the same time, however, the child's best interests may be somewhat broader than Ramsey is inclined to grant. Perhaps a parent, rather than focusing solely on physiological criteria, should be entitled to consider the emotional and psychological burdens (for the child) of the treatment. If the child's "best interests" must be narrowly construed because as a child he cannot determine his best interests in any broader sense, "medically indicated" must be construed broadly enough to include emotional and psychological burdens. And—at least until they prove themselves irresponsible and inattentive to their child's best interests—we should permit parents to make these decisions (not discoveries) for their children, and we should learn to live with the differences in their decisions just as we do with differences in decisions made by competent patients. That, at least, would be the ideal.

Perhaps, however, such an ideal—permitting families to decide, and decide differently, what treatments are too burdensome for their newborns, realizing that burdens are not only physiological—may today be unrealistic. In a day when people seem to find it almost impossible to separate burdens for the child from burdens for the rest of us, Ramsey may be wise to construe a medical indications policy rather narrowly. His may be, today, the only way to keep the child's best interests at the center of our concern. The fact of abuse suggests that possibilities I discuss as appropriate might only serve as the "thin edge of the wedge" to prepare us for judgments of comparative worth of lives. If so, Ramsey's narrowly construed medical indications policy would still offer the best rule of practice for medicine to follow.

In short, McCormick properly recognizes the importance of considering the burdens a treatment imposes when we are considering the best interests of an infant. But he encounters a host of difficulties by failing to appreciate that, in determining to refuse treatments for themselves, competent patients make a decision, not a discovery. Because this is the case, recourse to what reasonable people would decide can tell us little about what we should decide for an infant. All we can do is seek the best interests of that infant, and in this search Ramsey's medical indications policy is—if not fully satisfactory in every case—a rule of practice that embodies genuine moral discernment. Most of the time it will be wisest to do what is possible to preserve and enhance the life these infants have, in the hope that they may some day share with us the anxiety but also the joy of making decisions that shape their lives.

9

Withdrawing Food and Water

As infants we were given food and drink when we were too helpless to nourish ourselves. And for many of us a day will come before we die when we are once again too helpless to feed ourselves. If there is any way in which the living can stand by those who are not yet dead, it would seem to be through the continued provision of food and drink even when the struggle against disease has been lost. To continue to nourish the life of one who has been defeated in that battle is the last evidence we can offer that we are more than front-runners, that we are willing to love to the very point of death.

Today this intuitive reaction is being challenged. The President's Commission for the Study of Ethical Problems in Medicine and Biomedical and Behavioral Research has suggested that for patients with permanent loss of consciousness artificial-feeding interventions need not be continued.[1] A group of physicians writing in the *New England Journal of Medicine* has counseled doctors that, for irreversibly ill patients whose condition warrants nothing more aggressive than general nursing care, "naturally or artificially administered hydration and nutrition may be given or withheld, depending on the patient's comfort."[2]

Court decisions in cases like those of Claire Conroy in New Jersey or Clarence Herbert in California or Mary Hier in Massachusetts are contradictory,[3] but a consensus is gradually building toward the day when what we have already done in the case of some nondying infants with birth defects who were "allowed to die" by not being fed will become standard "treatment" for all patients who are permanently unconscious or suffering from severe and irreversible dementia. Those who defend this view stand ready with ethical arguments that nutrition and hydration are not "in the best interests" of such patients, but Daniel Callahan may have isolated the energizing force that is driving this consensus: "A denial of nutrition," he says, "may in the long run become the only effective way to make certain that a large number of biologically tenacious patients actually die."[4]

To the degree that this is true, however, the policy toward which we are moving is not merely one of "allowing to die": It is one of aiming to kill. *If* we are in fact heading in this direction, we should turn back before this policy corrupts our intellect and emotions and our capacity for moral reasoning. That stance I take to be a given, for which I shall not attempt to argue. Here I will consider only whether removal of artificial nutrition and hydration really does amount to no more than "allowing to die."

Why Feeding Is Not Medical Care

The argument for ceasing to feed seems strongest in cases of people suffering from a "persistent vegetative state," those (like Karen Quinlan) who have suffered an irreversible loss of consciousness. Sidney Wanzer and his physician colleagues suggest that in such circumstances "it is morally justifiable to withhold antibiotics and artificial nutrition and hydration, as well as other forms of life-sustaining treatment, allowing the patient to die." The President's Commission advises: "Since permanently unconscious patients will never be aware of nutrition, the only benefit to the patient of providing such increasingly burdensome interventions is sustaining the body to allow for a remote possibility of recovery. The sensitivities of the family and of care giving professionals ought to determine whether such interventions are made." Joanne Lynn, a physician at George Washington University, and James Childress, a professor of religious studies at the University of Virginia, believe that, "in these cases, it is very difficult to discern how any medical intervention can benefit or harm the patient."[5] But we need to ask whether the physicians are right to suggest that they seek only to allow the patient to die; whether the President's Commission has used language carefully enough in saying that nutrition and hydration of such persons are merely sustaining a *body;* whether Lynn and Childress may too readily have assumed that providing food and drink is *medical* treatment.

Should the provision of food and drink be regarded as *medical* care? It seems, rather, to be the sort of care that all human beings owe each other. All living beings need food and water in order to live, but such nourishment does not itself heal or cure disease. When we stop feeding the permanently unconscious patient, we are not withdrawing from the battle against any illness or disease; we are withholding the nourishment that sustains life.

The President's Commission does suggest that certain kinds of care remain mandatory for the permanently unconscious patient: "The awkward posture and lack of motion of unconscious patients often lead to pressure sores, and skin lesions are a major complication. Treatment and prevention of these problems is standard nursing care and should be provided." Yet it is hard to see why such services (turning the person regularly, giving alcohol rubs, and the like) are standard nursing care when feeding is not. Moreover, if feeding cannot benefit these patients, it is far from clear how they could experience bedsores as harm.

If this is true, we may have good reason to question whether the withdrawal of nutrition and hydration in such cases is properly characterized as stopping medical treatment in order to allow a patient to die. There are circumstances in which a plausible and helpful distinction can be made between killing and allowing to die, between an aim and a foreseen but unintended consequence. And sometimes it may make excellent moral sense to hold that we should cease to provide a now useless treatment, foreseeing but not intending that death will result. Such reasoning is also useful in the ethics of warfare, but there its use must be strictly controlled lest we simply unleash the bombs while "directing our intention" to a military target that could be attacked with far less firepower. Careful use of language is also necessary lest we talk about unconscious patients in ways that obscure our true aim.

Challenging those who have argued that it is no longer possible to distinguish between combatants and noncombatants in war, Michael Walzer has pointed out that "the relevant distinction is not between those who work for the war effort and those who do not, but between those who make what soldiers need to fight and those who make what they need to live, like the rest of us."[6]

Hence, farmers are not legitimate targets in war simply because they grow the food that soldiers need to live (and then to fight). The soldiers would need the food to live even if there were no war. Thus, as Paul Ramsey has observed, though an army may march upon its belly, bellies are not the target. It is an abuse of double-effect reasoning to justify cutting off the food supply of a nation as a way of stopping its soldiers. We could not properly say that we were aiming at the soldiers while merely foreseeing the deaths of the civilian population.

Nor can we, when withdrawing food from the permanently unconscious person, properly claim that our intention is to cease useless treatment for a dying patient. These patients are not dying, and we cease no treatment aimed at disease; rather, we withdraw the nourishment that sustains all human beings whether healthy or ill, and we do so when the only result of our action can be death. At what, other than that death, could we be aiming?

One might argue that the same could be said of turning off a respirator, but the situations are somewhat different. Remove a person from a respirator and he may die—but, then, he may also surprise us and continue to breathe spontaneously. We test to see if the patient can breathe. If he does, it is not our task—unless we are aiming at his death—now to smother him (or to stop feeding him). But deprive a person of food and water and she will die as surely as if we had administered a lethal drug, and it is hard to claim that we did not aim at her death.

I am unable—and this is a lack of insight, not of space—to say more about the analogy between eating and breathing. Clearly, air is as essential to life as food. We might wonder, therefore, whether provision of air is not also more than medical treatment. What justification could there be, then, for turning off a respirator? If the person's death, due to the progress of a disease, is irreversibly and imminently at hand, then continued assistance with respiration may now be useless. But if the person is not going to die from any disease but, instead, simply needs assistance with breathing because of some injury, it is less clear to me why such assistance should not be given. More than this I am unable to say. I repeat, however, that to remove a respirator is not necessarily to aim at death; one will not go on to kill the patient who manages to breathe spontaneously. But it is difficult for me to construe removal of nutrition for permanently unconscious patients in any other way. Perhaps we only wish them dead or think they would be better off dead. There are circumstances in which such a thought is understandable. But it would still be wrong to enact that wish by aiming at their death.

Separating Personhood and Body

Suppose we were to accept the view that provision of food and water is properly termed medical treatment. Is there good reason to withhold this treatment from permanently unconscious patients? A treatment refusal needs to be justified either on the ground that the treatment is (or has now become) useless, or that the treatment (though perhaps still useful) is excessively burdensome for the patient. Still taking as our focus the permanently unconscious patient, we can consider, first, whether feeding is useless. There could be occasions on which artificial feeding would be futile. Lynn and Childress offer instances of patients who simply cannot be fed effectively, but they are not cases of permanently unconscious patients.

Yet, for many people the uselessness of feeding the permanently unconscious seems self-evident. Why? Probably because they suppose that the nourishment we provide is, in the words of the President's Commission, doing no more than "sustaining the body." But we should pause before separating personhood and body so decisively. When considering other topics (care of the environment, for example) we are eager to criticize a dualism that divorces human reason and consciousness from the larger world of nature. Why not here? We can know people—of all ranges of cognitive capacity—only as they are embodied; there is no other "person" for whom we might care. Such care is not useless if it "only" preserves bodily life but does not restore cognitive capacities. Even if it is less than we wish could be accomplished, it remains care for the embodied person.

Some will object to characterizing as persons those who lack the capacity or even the potential for self-awareness, for envisioning a future for themselves, for relating to other selves. I am not fully persuaded that speaking of "persons" in such contexts is mistaken, but the point can be made without using that language. Human nature has a capacity to know, to be self-aware, and to relate to others. We can share in that human nature even though we may not yet or no longer exercise all the functions of which it is capable. We share in it simply by virtue of being born into the human species. We could describe as persons all individuals sharing our common nature, all members of the species. Or we could ascribe personhood only to those human beings presently capable of exercising the characteristic human functions.

I think it better—primarily because it is far less dualistic—to understand personhood as an endowment that comes with our nature, even if at some stages of life we are unable to exercise characteristic human capacities. But the point can be made, if anyone wishes, by talking of embodied human beings rather than embodied persons. To be a human being one need not presently be exercising or be capable of exercising the functions characteristic of consciousness. Those are capacities of human nature; they are not functions that all human beings exercise. It is human beings, not just persons in that more restricted sense, whose death should not be our aim. And if this view is characterized as an objectionable "speciesism," I can only reply that at least it is not one more way by which the strong and gifted in our world rid themselves of the weak, and it does not fall prey to that abstraction by which we reify consciousness and separate it from the body.

The permanently unconscious are not dying subjects who should simply be allowed to die. But they will, of course, die if we aim at their death by ceasing to feed them. If we are not going to feed them because that would be nothing more than sustaining a body, why not bury them at once? No one, I think, recommends that. But if, then, they are still living beings who ought not to be buried, the nourishment that all human beings need to live ought not to be denied them. When we permit ourselves to think that care is useless if it preserves the life of the embodied human being without restoring cognitive capacity, we fall victim to the old delusion that we have failed if we cannot *cure* and that there is, then, little point to continued *care*. David Smith, a professor of religious studies at the University of Indiana, has suggested that I might be mistaken in describing the comatose person as a "nondying" patient. At least in some cases, he believes, lapsing into permanent coma might be a sign that a person is trying to die. Thus, though a comatose state would not itself be sufficient reason to characterize someone as dying, it might be one of several conditions that, taken together, would be sufficient. This is a reasonable suggestion, and it might enable us to distinguish different sorts of comatose patients—the dying, for whom feeding might be useless; the nondying, for whom it would not. Even then, however, I would still be troubled by the worry I raised earlier: whether food and drink are really medical treatment that should be withdrawn when it becomes useless.

Even when care is not useless it may be so burdensome that it should be dispensed with. When that is the case, we can honestly say—and it makes good moral sense to say—that our aim is to relieve the person of a burden, with the foreseen but unintended effect of a hastened death. We should note, however, that this line of argument *cannot* be applied to the cases of the permanently unconscious. Other patients—those, for example, with fairly severe dementia—may be made afraid and uncomfortable by artificial nutrition and hydration. But this can hardly be true of the permanently unconscious. It seems unlikely that they experience as burdensome the care involved in feeding them.

Even for severely demented patients who retain some consciousness, we should be certain that we are considering the burden of continued existence itself. In the case of Claire Conroy, for example, the trial judge suggested that her life (not simply the intervention needed to feed her) had become "impossibly and permanently burdensome." That is a judgment, I think, that no one should make for another; indeed, it is hard to know exactly how one would do so. Besides, it seems evident that if the burden involved is her continued life the point of ceasing to feed is that we aim at relieving her of that burden—that is, we aim to kill.

Having said that, I am quite ready to grant that the burden of the feeding itself may sometimes be so excessive that it is not warranted. Lynn and Childress offer examples, some of which seem persuasive. If, however, we want to assess the burden of the treatment, we should certainly not dispense with nutrition and hydration until a reasonable trial period has demonstrated that the person truly finds such care excessively burdensome.

In short, if we focus our attention on irreversibly ill adults for whom general nursing care but no more seems appropriate, we can say the following: First, when the person is permanently unconscious, the care involved in feeding can hardly be experienced as burdensome. Neither can such care be described as useless, since it preserves the life of the embodied human being (who is not a dying patient). Second, when the person is conscious but severely and irreversibly demented, the care involved in feeding, though not useless, *may* be so burdensome that it should cease. This requires demonstration during a trial period, however, and the judgment is quite different from concluding that the person's life has become too burdensome to preserve. Third, for both sorts of patients the care involved in feeding is not, in any strict sense, medical treatment, even if provided in a hospital. It gives what all need to live; it is treatment of no particular disease; and its cessation means certain death, a death at which we can only be said to aim, whatever our motive.

That we should continue to feed the permanently unconscious still seems obvious to some people, even as it was to Karen Quinlan's father at the time he sought removal of her respirator. It has not always seemed so to me, but it does now. For the permanently unconscious person, feeding is neither useless nor excessively burdensome. It is ordinary human care and is not given as treatment for any life-threatening disease. Since this is true, a decision not to offer such care can enact only one intention: to take the life of the unconscious person.

I have offered no arguments here to prove that such a life-taking intention and aim would be morally wrong, though I believe it is and that to embrace such an aim would be corrupting. If we can face the fact that withdrawing the nourishment of such persons is, indeed, aiming to kill, I am hopeful (though not altogether confident) that the more fundamental principle will not need to be argued. Let us hope that this is the case, since that more basic principle is not one that can be argued *to;* rather, all useful moral argument must proceed *from* the conviction that it is wrong to aim to kill the innocent.

Part Four
Community

10

Marital Community

Among the bonds that connect human lives, perhaps the most central is the community of marriage. Not all marry, and not all need to marry. Human fulfillment is quite possible apart from marriage or any expression of genital sexuality. And yet, having said that, it remains true that the complete giving and receiving that marriage makes possible between a man and a woman is central to human life and is the typical expression of our co-humanity, our creation as male and female. Within the Christian era, probably no human relationship has been subjected to more scrutiny; certainly none has received the sustained theological reflection that marriage has.

Christians have often disagreed about matters connected with sexuality and marriage. They have valued differently the celibate life; they have debated the sacramental character of marriage; they have reached different conclusions about the possibility and permissibility of divorce; they have differed about the morality of contraceptive intercourse. At the same time, Christian understanding of marital community has remained in many respects stable, and the areas of disagreement have not destroyed common understanding of the bond. Whether this remains true today is hard to say. Contemporary Christian discussion of sexuality and marriage has sometimes—and quite self-consciously—rung the changes on different themes. The book that, within the last decade, has best reflected this changed climate may be James Nelson's *Embodiment:*

An Approach to Sexuality and Christian Theology.[1] It has been widely noted and, usually, applauded. Its importance does not lie in any particular originality; indeed, it is finally unsatisfying in its eclecticism. But this very lack of originality makes it useful as a touchstone. The book faithfully reflects the present state of much Christian talk about sexuality and marriage. By considering some of Nelson's claims, we give ourselves an opportunity to reconsider the nature of marital community. We will look first at his discussion of sexuality, then at what he says about marital fidelity, and finally at his treatment of several sexual variations.

Sexuality: Dualism and Duality

Nelson contends that our experience of ourselves as sexual beings has been permeated and distorted by two dualisms: (1) a split between self and body in which the "real self" has been regarded as incorporeal, and (2) a sexist dualism in which women have been dominated by men. Both dualisms stem from the still more fundamental alienation of human beings from God. It is important to characterize accurately the distinction between *dualism* and *duality*—especially since Nelson himself does not always observe it. Dualism occurs when two different elements that may live together in harmony do not, but, instead, are frequently in conflict and (at best) "live together in an uneasy truce" (p. 37). A duality, or polarity, on the other hand, holds together in harmonious and creative union two disparate elements—holds them together without obliterating their separateness.

There are important lessons to be learned from Nelson's discussion of the body/self dualism. There is also a good bit to be criticized. We are, he suggests, often alienated from our bodies.

(It may seem strange to us to say, "I am my body," even though we have read time and again that we are created "from the dust of the ground.") As a result, we may regard fleshly relationships as less important than a theology that affirms the goodness of God's creation should. To give a few examples (which are mine, not Nelson's, but with which he ought to concur if he seriously wishes to avoid a body/self dualism): Only a dualistic age could (1) imagine that sexual encounters between persons not committed to a permanent union are "casual" since a bodily commitment need not involve the person; (2) experiment on patients without their consent; (3) acquiesce in talk of a woman's body as a kind of property that she owns.

The body/self dualism arises (and recurs) in our history because of sin, because nature and spirit have quarreled within the human person. When in our sin we inject disorder into the creation by becoming rebels against God, that disorder and rebellion work themselves out in our lives, in our "body-selves." These two aspects of our one person no longer live in creative harmony but, instead, in conflict. We get dualism rather than duality. Indeed, none of us has ever experienced any life except one permeated by the conflict of nature and spirit within the self, and we will not fully *experience* such a redeemed existence (and be fully at home in our bodies) within history.

The fact that this is the case—that, to put it in traditional terms, we are born in sin and remain, at best, justified sinners in this life—raises a crucial problem that Nelson never satisfactorily addresses. The personal, self-transcending self and the physical body—spirit and nature—have quarreled. They are no longer in harmony. How then are we to know what right order within the self would be like? If there were only a *duality* between nature and spirit rather than a *dualism,* what sort of creatures would we be? Clearly, Nelson has some notion of what we would be like. He can write that "central to the image of God in which we are created is the will to communion. We are social beings through and through. We are nurtured into our humanness in community, and we have some deep, often unarticulated, sense that loving communion is our intended and ultimate destiny" (p. 104). Talk about mutuality and communion remains unhelpfully vague, however, especially when Nelson does not show us how it is connected to the importance of "embodiment." And without greater clarity we will not know when we are confronting a duality, which presumably should be affirmed, and when we are confronting a dualism, which presumably should not. One begins to fear in reading Nelson that, under the guise of statements, true enough in themselves, about the historical character of human existence, we may begin to take contemporary ideas of human fulfillment as our image of a redeemed human community.

The failure clearly to distinguish dualism from duality may explain the fact that Nelson has little—and certainly little that is positive—to say about the ascetic tradition in Christian history. He assumes, one suspects, that asceticism is an expression of the objectionable dualism between body and self. Indeed, he writes that "the ascetic experiences the body as a dangerous, alien force to be sternly controlled, even crushed into submission" (p. 40). But what if asceticism is a reaction to, rather than an expression of, body/self dualism? If spirit and nature have quarreled within the self, then at least on some occasions the body may in fact be a dangerous force in need of stern control. Nelson can ignore this possibility only because he presumes he knows what a harmoniously integrated "body-self" would be like. But he does not. None of us does. We do, though, know that a good bit of mortification of the bodily passions (but also, of course, of the spiritual passions) could be required along the way to becoming such a harmonious body-self. Screwtape writes to Wormwood about God: "He's a hedonist at heart. All those fasts and vigils and stakes and crosses are only a facade. Or only like foam on the seashore. Out at sea, out in His sea, there is pleasure, and more pleasure. He makes no secret of it; at His right hand are 'pleasures forevermore.' "[2] Nevertheless—and this is the cardinal truth that the ascetic sees—the way to those pleasures may, at least for some, be the way of renunciation. We can say that with far more certainty than we can say what a harmoniously integrated body-self would be or do.

None of this should obscure the fundamental point Nelson makes. Nature and spirit *have* quarreled; we *are* alienated from our bodies; we *are* in need of healing. He suggests that, if some Sunday a preacher were to announce as his text Paul's exhortation that we present our bodies a living sacrifice to God, we would probably hear only an injunction to discipline our bodily life rather than a call to offer the whole of it, including its pleasures, in thanks to God (p. 41). Such alienation from our physical, fleshly existence is a result of sin and calls for healing.

The other sort of dualism that Nelson discusses is sexist dualism—in which men and women relate to one another in patterns of submission and domination. This dualism is also a result of the sinful self's alienation from God. It is after the fall that God tells the woman that her desire will be to her husband who will rule over her.

Here again, however, to recognize the dualism is not to recognize what a right relation between male and female would be. If communion in love is to remain the ideal, a duality must be affirmed even while dualism is rejected. Those joined in a bond of mutual love are those who are different—other—and whose individuality is not obliterated or merged into an undifferentiated oneness. Our task, then, is not to transcend the male-female duality but to learn how to live it: to find a relationship in which men and women, retaining their otherness, live together in harmony. As with body/self dualism, we must ask what such a harmonious relationship would be like and how we know where to draw the line between rejected dualism and affirmed duality. On this question Nelson is once more unconvincing.

He distinguishes the biological category of sex (male/female) from gender (masculine/feminine) and stresses that the latter is as much a social and cultural phenomenon as a biological one. That is, our sense of self as masculine or feminine is not simply determined by our biological maleness or femaleness. And he cites data suggesting that, if a male child is reared as a member of the female sex, his gender identity will be feminine (p. 59). From such data Nelson concludes that we ought not to assume that masculine characteristics are appropriate only to males and feminine characteristics only to females. Instead, he affirms the ideal of the androgynous personality that unites masculine and feminine characteristics in one person, whether male or female. If this is the ideal, one wonders what has become of "embodiment." For this is only a new version of body/self alienation. According to Nelson, gender orientation ought to be unrelated to one's biological sexual identity; that is, it ought to be alike for (biological) males and females. The permitted duality seems to boil down simply to the fact that women bear children and men do not. To regard any other masculine or feminine characteristics as peculiarly appropriate to men or women would be the rejected dualism. It is clear that on this view body has little or nothing to do with personhood. No doubt it is true that we cannot say precisely what a right relation between gender identity and biological sexuality would be like, but there must be some relation between the two if the biological self is to be related to the personal self. The ideal of the androgynous personality makes the biological differentiation unimportant to one's real self—and Nelson himself becomes a dualist!

We should do as Nelson says—not as he does. The task of ethical reflection—indeed, the task of Christian men and women—is to find moral significance *within* the distinctions of finite, embodied human life. Thus, for example, Lisa Sowle Cahill writes: "To say basic physical forms of existence have no cognitive or affective implications seems dualistic. It separates humanity from its own biological concreteness and from other animal species. This fragmentation runs counter to our attempts on other fronts to demonstrate the unity of body and spirit and the interdependence of humanity and the rest of nature."[3] Understanding our task in this way does not lead Cahill to imagine that she can unfold fully the moral significance of sexual differentiation. But it permits her to hold that—although the meaning of masculinity and femininity goes beyond biological distinctions—the differentiation of male and female "must take some concrete forms."[4] The androgynous ideal is, then, simply a new version of "the liberal ideal of the autonomous agent, unconstrained—indeed undefined—by any significant communal or physical boundaries."[5] At best such autonomous agents may manage to come together in contractual associations of one sort or another; however, their being will not be defined by their creation as male and female. The ideal of the androgynous personality does not offer a way for men and women, despite their otherness, to live in fellowship; instead, it seeks to transcend that otherness. This is not the way to overcome dualism, nor is it the way to sustain duality in the bond of male and female. If we cannot at present say precisely what form or forms that duality ought to take, we can at least recognize the search for such forms as a task laid upon us.

Marital Fidelity

As we turn more directly to consider the marital bond, it may be worthwhile to begin with a point not about marriage but about ethical reasoning. In discussing the factors to be considered in evaluating our actions, Nelson (in quite standard fashion) distinguishes motive, intention, the nature of the act itself, and the act's consequences (p. 128). The third of these, however, turns out to be of little significance (and here again Nelson's importance lies largely in the fact that he simply mirrors a good bit of contemporary ethical thought). He writes that he finds it "extremely difficult to label whole classes of acts as inherently right or wrong, since moral quality hinges so heavily on what is being communicated to the persons involved in the particular relationship and context" (p. 128). That is to say, the moral quality of the action depends primarily on motive and intention.

Again, however, one must ask what has become of the ideal of "embodiment." Has it no effect on our understanding of ethical theory? How can a thinker who hopes to overcome dualism by emphasizing embodiment imagine that we should determine the intention of an action (that is, the aim of the agent) without making quite central the physical nature of the act? Nelson has not here taken his talk of "embodiment" seriously enough. It would have been far more creative and radical—as well as considerably closer to the truth—had Nelson suggested that any ethicist who took his understanding of embodiment seriously would have to consider the physical nature of the act as a centrally important factor in determining the agent's aim. It would be radical if Nelson had said that an act of intercourse with someone else's spouse must necessarily aim at rupturing the bond of commitment with one's own spouse. But such a radical questioning of our dualistic culture is not Nelson's style, and one is led to wonder whether the category of embodiment has had any transforming effect on the manner of his ethical reflection.

The form or forms that marriage takes ought to be "congruent with the authentic needs of persons" (p. 143). This is the basic premise from which Nelson proceeds to examine the requirement of fidelity within marriage. The authentic needs of persons turn out to be rather difficult to pin down, however. Because we are finite, historical beings it is inappropriate, Nelson suggests, to "absolutize" any form of institutional life on earth, including marriage. That this is surely true of much within the marital community we may gladly grant. But the assumption that "absolutizing" fidelity would be somehow idolatrous is a curious one. We could just as easily describe it as an attempt to be true to the image of absolute love as it has become incarnate and historical in Jesus of Nazareth, and we could say that nothing less than such fidelity could finally be "congruent with the authentic needs of persons."

In *Too Far to Go,* John Updike tells the story of the disintegration of the marriage of Joan and Richard Maple. In the book's foreword Updike reflects upon the significance of such an ending. "That a marriage ends is less than ideal; but all things end under heaven, and if temporality is held to be invalidating, then nothing real succeeds."[6] Like Nelson's unwillingness to "absolutize" fidelity, this might seem a wise attempt to come to terms with human finitude, yet it may not be what it seems. For the human being is two-sided: finite, but also made for the Eternal One. And the glory and terror of marriage is that in it we attempt to hold together these two sides of our nature in a single commitment. We permit the Eternal to touch and transform our commitment. The "real" is not the temporal taken by itself, but the temporal bond transformed by divine love. For example, Richard Maple at one point reflects that he could not really be himself in this transient, finite existence. "In death, he felt, . . . he would grow to his true size."[7] Only in death can he really be himself, because only then can he be sure that he will not change. What Richard cannot manage, however, is to find an unchanging fidelity within time. And since he cannot, he must long for death. The paradox is, therefore, that his inability to find the Eternal within time turns out to invalidate his experience of time itself—leaves him feeling that he cannot be himself within time. The stories suggest a truth deeper than the moral the author finds in them. The complexity of our nature must be fully respected. We are constituted by our finite attachments and commitments, but they cannot stand alone. They must be open to and drawn into the transforming power of God's love.

Fidelity is, therefore, central in the bond of marriage, and Nelson provides a clear account of the reasons Christian thinkers have given to explain its importance (pp. 143ff.). These are primarily four:

(1) Straightforward biblical warrants seem to require such fidelity.

(2) Marriage is thought of as a one-flesh union in which a complete sharing—also over time—of life with life is to take place.

(3) The pattern of Christ's own faithfulness is held up as the ideal for Christian marriage.

(4) It is common Christian conviction that the union of a man and woman, at least in the totality of their conjugal acts, should be open to the procreative purpose that human sexuality serves; and this, in turn, requires a marital bond capable of receiving and rearing children.

The strength of these claims is acknowledged by Nelson, and, indeed, it seems clear that he is himself committed to the worth and importance of fidelity. He argues, nevertheless, that the various stresses and strains to which the family in our society is subject require that we take a closer look at what marriage has become. Many couples may today feel compelled to choose between (1) sexual exclusivity and (2) marital permanence. That is, spouses today may feel a need to grow beyond the confines of their marital union in order to realize themselves fully as human beings. Under such circumstances the only way to maintain an ongoing, permanent marital union may be to admit the possibility that genital relationships with partners other than the spouse might be permissible. Not to grant that possibility, to insist instead on sexual exclusivity within marriage, may only destroy the ideal of permanence in marriage. Nelson seems to argue that this kind of trade-off, though perhaps less than optimally desirable, may be the best we can manage.

We need not deny, I suppose, that it would be better to retain marital permanence than to lose both it and sexual exclusivity. And indeed, Christian pastors in their counseling may sometimes have to reckon with that harsh fact. But Nelson is not offering counsel to a troubled marriage; he is writing ethics. And in that undertaking the best he can offer is a "presumptive rule" in favor of general exclusivity, a rule of thumb that can admit of exceptions (p. 151). Will that be enough to retain what is essential in the Christian understanding of marriage? We may have our doubts. We may doubt, even, whether it does full justice to Nelson's own category of embodiment. This view of fidelity, it should be obvious, isolates the physical, genital union from the fullest personal relationship. Nelson here rejects the view (articulated by D. S. Bailey and others) that the very act of intercourse itself is always of importance for the person, not just for a body alienated from the self (pp. 371f.). By contrast, Nelson emphasizes the significance the partners themselves *attach* to the act. Perhaps he is correct and Bailey incorrect, but surely it is Bailey and not Nelson who is taking embodiment more seriously. Surely it is Nelson and not Bailey who is flirting with a body/self dualism.

Marriage, within the Christian tradition, is to serve a healing purpose. It is, among other things, a divine ordinance intended to bring our wayward desires and passions under control, intended to begin to shape them in accord with the pattern of God's faithfulness. To be sure, the need for human fulfillment is not to be ignored, but we know at least this much about authentic humanity: It must be a growing up into Christ. Maturity is measured by the full stature of Christ, who was faithful in every circumstance of life, who sought not his own fulfillment but went the way of the cross, and who, in so doing, was vindicated by the Father. The way to human fulfillment in a sinful world may be more indirect than many people today believe, and though he knows and cites the passage, Nelson has not let his understanding of human fulfillment be shaped sufficiently by the truth that one finds life by losing it.

A "presumptive rule" in favor of fidelity is not likely to be sufficient to fulfill the healing purpose of marriage. It can only mean, "I promise . . . unless and until new possibilities for growth and self-realization lead me to a new partner." If that is the promise the church wishes to witness and to which it wants to give its blessing, it ought to be spoken in precisely such language. That kind of promise, however, will never discipline the desires of sinful human beings. It will not serve the healing that all children of Adam need.

Sexual Variations

Nelson's discussion of sexual variations is informed, sober, and compassionate. It ought also, in certain fundamental ways, to be rejected. Here I explore only his discussion of masturbation and homosexuality.

Condemnations of masturbation have certainly been overdone within Christian history, and it becomes an important moral problem only when certain claims—which Nelson, unfortunately, endorses—are made. He stresses that the act of masturbation may have a different significance in different contexts. Its significance for the adolescent exploring his or her identity and its significance for the radical feminist who sees it as a rejection of the male are, for example, quite different. To say that the quality of the act may be different in such circumstances and require richly nuanced moral judgments seems reasonable.

Nelson moves considerably beyond this, however, and accepts certain judgments that Christian thought ought to condemn. Thus, he gives his approval to the view that in masturbation one learns the truth that the self can be simultaneously lover and beloved (pp. 171f.). He quotes approvingly the view that "there is great freedom in knowing that one can be whole in one's inner life, and that this wholeness need not depend absolutely upon a relationship with another person" (p. 172). That "wholeness" is, we should note, what Christians have traditionally called hell: positing an independence in which one can live for the self alone. It is difficult to say what has happened here to Nelson's stated view that we are beings made for communion with one another. He is so concerned to stress that self-affirmation is a necessary component of human fulfillment that he forgets that there is, for Christian thought, no self that can be whole in itself apart from God and the neighbor. Even more striking is his suggestion that the physiological pleasure of orgasm in masturbation may be a way of affirming the goodness of the body-self, an affirmation that "there can be a communion within which is not unrelated to the communion of self with others, world, and God" (p. 173). And yet, this communion is precisely willed as unrelated to all others. It might, I suspect, be more appropriately labeled "idolatry."

It would be far healthier to engage in masturbation simply for the purpose of physical release and pleasure than to engage in it as a way of affirming the wholeness, goodness, and independence of one's body-self. The former does not involve a rejection of community with others as essential to human fulfillment; it simply settles for a lower, purely physical, pleasure. Only when the act is given a personal, symbolic significance like that which Nelson suggests does it make room for the sin of human pride to assert itself. It is precisely when masturbation is placed into the human context and given the significance Nelson gives it that it becomes dangerous, for then it is a deliberate step away from the purpose and destination for which we are created.

An entire chapter of Nelson's book is devoted to the issue of homosexuality, and he is surely not mistaken in recognizing that it has become a central issue for moral reflection within the church. He makes the now common and important distinction between homosexual acts and a homosexual orientation and rightly recognizes that one could hardly be blamed morally for the latter. When he moves beyond this, however, to claim that genital acts engaged

in by those of homosexual orientation ought not to be condemned, his discussion is less satisfactory. It is correct to say that
there are people for whom a homosexual orientation has always
seemed natural, who have always experienced themselves as sexual
beings in this way. We understand what Nelson means, therefore,
in saying that this orientation is a part of "their nature" and that
such persons are not those whom Paul (in Romans 1) condemns
as engaging in "unnatural" acts (p. 186).

Nevertheless, "nature" is, as Nelson ought to know, a word to
conjure with. It may mean simply "what is given"—and it is in this
sense that Nelson uses the term. But "nature" may also mean what
is appropriate to a creature of a certain kind, not just what is given
in nature. Simply to say (rightly) that one cannot be blamed for a
homosexual orientation one did not choose is not to say that such
an orientation ought to be affirmed as appropriate or in accord
with the Creator's will for human life. Considerably more than
some conjuring with the word "natural" will be needed.

In the course of providing a (very helpful) typology of positions
within the church with respect to homosexuality, Nelson indicates
the basis for his own judgment that homosexual acts and orientation ought to receive "full acceptance" within the church. He
asserts once again the historical character of human existence, the
fact that our nature is not unchangeable. Hence, the cultural significance with which we once surrounded human sexuality need
not be lasting. In a new context that physical act may take on a
different significance; it may even point the way to a new mode of
fulfillment and growth.

It is true enough that human nature as we know it, corrupted
by sin, cannot be normative. What is normative is the nature to
which God summons us. Nelson wishes to characterize that nature toward which we are summoned simply in terms of mutuality, a characterization that takes little account of the importance of
embodiment. It is as male and female that humanity is created in
the image of God. The mutuality for which we are destined is a

loving union of those who are *other*. And for creatures who are finite, historical, and earthly—for embodied human beings—that otherness has a biological grounding. Homosexual acts are forbidden precisely because lover and beloved are, biologically, not sufficiently other. The relationship approaches too closely the forbidden love of self.

This is the underlying warrant for the consistent condemnation of homosexual acts within Christian tradition. (Another important reason, also grounded in our embodied character, is the obviously nonprocreative character of the homosexual relationship.) Perhaps this view is mistaken, as Nelson thinks it is, but we should note that it is a view that takes our embodied character with full seriousness. We are not just spirits, beings who create worlds of meaning and significance and symbol—we are creatures *in the flesh*. What Nelson needs to show, and has not shown, is that he can reject this view without reaffirming the body/self dualism he deplores in the opening chapters of his book.

To repeat what was said at the outset: Nelson's book is worth our consideration precisely because in what it says about sexuality and the marriage bond he is *not* original. He voices views that are current and commonly held within Christendom. The book's weakness lies largely in the fact that its attack on dualism does not seem really to have penetrated to the center of Nelson's moral reasoning. The central problem with which Nelson is wrestling— the compresence of nature and spirit, physical and personal, within the human being—is a crucial one for Christian thought about marriage, and it is not an easy problem. Since nature and spirit have quarreled, the only humanity we experience is one in which these two do not exist in the harmony God willed. To learn what right order within the self and within the marital bond would look like it will be necessary to make the biblical story of creation and redemption more central in moral reflection than Nelson has done. In doing that we may regain and renew a common Christian understanding of the marital bond.

11

Political Community

We too easily forget that, however much liberal individualism may be a product of our modern, industrialized world, it is also the product of Christendom. If there is truth in St. Augustine's assertion that the human heart is restless until it rests in God, the human person can never belong entirely to any historical community, and human virtue can never be defined sufficiently in terms of good citizenship.

That this is a lesson too easily forgotten even by sensitive interpreters of our Western tradition is evident in George Will's recent statement of his theory of politics.[1] The book's preface is preceded by an epigraph quoting a famous passage from Cicero:

> Well, then, a commonwealth is the property of a people. But a people is not any collection of human beings brought together in any sort of way, but an assemblage of people in large numbers associated in an agreement with respect to justice and a partnership for the common good. The first cause of such an association is not so much the weakness of the individual as a certain social spirit which nature has implanted in man.

When, then, on the very first page of the first chapter Will describes his undertaking as "Augustinian," the reader may anticipate that Cicero is to be Will's foil. For the passage Will quotes from Cicero is famous primarily because of Augustine's treatment of it in his *City of God*. Augustine first cites Cicero's definition of a commonwealth in II,21, and says that later, "God willing," he will attempt to show that according to Cicero's definition Rome itself was never a true commonwealth. Pages—and years!—later, in XIX,21, Augustine returns to his promise. He argues that, if a commonwealth requires people agreed with respect to justice, there can be no commonwealth where God is not loved above all else. And, Augustine knows, there are no such political communities. He therefore proposes a more reasonable definition, one which demythologizes politics and undercuts the pretensions of government. A people is simply "a multitude of reasonable beings voluntarily associated in the pursuit of common interests" (XIX,24). Commonwealths will be better or worse according as the interests that unite their people are better or worse. But when subjected to theological scrutiny, all political communities, even the very best, are analogous to bands of robbers.

> The answer which a captured pirate gave to the celebrated Alexander the Great was perfectly accurate and correct. When that king asked the man what he meant by infesting the sea, he boldly replied: "What you mean by warring on the whole world. I do my fighting on a tiny ship, and they call me a pirate; you do yours with a large fleet, and they call you Commander." (IV,4)

That is what Augustine does to Cicero's definition of a commonwealth. And we may be surprised, therefore, that Will's "Augustinian" undertaking should be to argue that "statecraft is soulcraft." "Politics should," he writes, "share one purpose with religion: the steady emancipation of the individual through the education of his passions" (p. 27). Augustine demythologized the political. Our task, Will writes, is to "reclaim for politics a properly great and stately jurisdiction" (p. 22). Virtue Will defines as "good citizenship" (p. 134). For Augustine the virtue of the very best of citizens—of a Regulus (I,15)—was only splendid vice.

That George Will's undertaking is not, in the most important sense, Augustinian does not mean that he is not an acute and thoughtful observer of the society in which we live. That the individualism of our world often seems destructive, that we demonstrate little willingness to sacrifice private desires for public ends—these contentions of his would be hard to deny. We need, therefore, to think carefully about the relation of individual and community. And it soon becomes clear that this is also to think about the relation of ethics and politics.

I will develop the thesis, certainly not original with me, that good ethics may not be good politics. That, in particular, some things we may need to say (ethically) about the relation of persons and their communities are dangerous as guides to political life. That what is best politically probably falls short of our highest moral ideals. I intend, that is, an Augustinian undertaking. Or, one could say, I hope to support a version of the liberal tradition in Western political thought. At the conclusion of his famous essay "Two Concepts of Liberty," Isaiah Berlin suggests that the civilized person is one who recognizes the (merely) relative validity of his convictions, yet stands by them. And Berlin writes: "To demand more than this is perhaps a deep and incurable metaphysical need; but to allow it to determine one's practice is a symptom of an equally deep, and more dangerous, moral and political immaturity."[2] We have what may justly be called a deep metaphysical need to become persons of a certain sort, virtuous selves. And there is truth to the claim (made, for example, by George Will) that such virtue can be developed only in communities of a certain sort. But there is also truth—or so I will argue—in the claim that such communities are dangerous.

To develop this argument I will draw upon the thought of Isaiah Berlin and of Michael Walzer, each a perceptive political theorist. I offer no adequate interpretation of their views but will simply use them—the one, a great defender of liberty; the other, an advocate of fraternal solidarity—to help sketch three ways of understanding the relation between individuals and their political communities. Each is, of course, an ideal type that exists nowhere, yet the sketch will call to our attention certain features of life in community. Each type has its own understanding of virtue and of the relation between freedom and virtue. Each has its own view of the relative importance of participation in the common life and sacrifice for that common life. Each presumes a view about the relation of ethics and politics. The first may be said to be one form—but only one—of the liberal tradition. The second is a form of that ancient tradition—a fraternal understanding of public life—that Will suggests we recapture. The third is also a form of the liberal tradition, but one tinged with Augustinian presuppositions.[3]

Politics Without Ethics: The Night-Watchman State

The point of government may be the provision of a system of rules by which citizens order their associations with each other. In that case, the political community—as a community—is going nowhere in particular, has no particular goal or mission in life. As Michael Walzer writes, "a liberal nation can have no collective purpose."[4] The freedom important in such a community is the freedom to pursue one's private purposes, whatever they may be, as long as they are pursued within the boundaries established by the shared system of rules.

Two different sorts of ethical premises may underlie such a conception of government—one emphasized more by Walzer, the other by Berlin. But both have been central in the liberal tradition. We may, on the one hand, emphasize that selves are "bundles of interests," necessarily clashing with each other. As Walzer puts it, in a fine development of a Hobbesian metaphor, "in a race, one has competitors, not colleagues or comrades" (RP, 294). Alternatively, we may think of the self not as a bundle of interests but as a "repository of imaginative possibilities."[5] That is, we may emphasize not the clash of interests but the irreducible plurality of ends in life. Isaiah Berlin notes, in an essay on John Stuart Mill, that Mill's commitment must (or should) have been not to liberty as a means to other ends but as a good desirable in its own right. For example, suppose we defend freedom as a means to the emergence of truth. It is arguable that a love of truth is as likely to emerge in a strictly disciplined society as in a more liberal, tolerant one. We may, of course, fondly hope that freedom will prove the way to truth, but if it does not, a liberal like Mill would have to choose between freedom and truth (FEL, 128).

That freedom will prove the way to virtue is perhaps even less likely. Indeed, for this first ideal type, it will be hard to say much about virtue. If we talk of it at all, it is likely to be what Walzer terms "civility": social virtues such as orderliness and politeness (RP, 59). The political community recognizes a plurality of forms of the good life and must therefore have difficulty nourishing and sustaining any particular set of virtues. Content to establish boundaries that control conflicts of interest among citizens, government must necessarily aim at a kind of lowest-common-denominator virtue.

This may not seem bad. We might suggest that inculcating "higher" visions of virtue must be the task of smaller groups within the community. But there is danger in what we may picture as a "seepage" problem. When enshrined at the center of our public consciousness is the minimal virtue that asks only civility, when our common life acknowledges a plurality of forms of the good life and the need for freedom to pursue our private visions of the good life—when these are the beliefs upon which our community is founded—it will be difficult to prevent a belief in the primacy of private interests from seeping down into and dominating our understanding of virtue. Serious moral education, serious training in virtue, may then become difficult to sustain. We may even have difficulty sustaining the common life of smaller groups upon which we are relying to transmit those "higher" elements of our moral vision.

In this community participation in public life can scarcely be of any great value. In fact, it is more likely to be an onerous chore—necessary perhaps on occasion, but hardly the sort of activity to which one is devoted. Hence, Isaiah Berlin notes that, for those who value primarily the freedom to pursue their private visions, *self*-government may be of relatively little importance. Such a view has been memorably expressed by Michael Oakeshott: "Politics is a second-rate form of activity . . . at once corrupting to the soul and fatiguing to the mind, the activity either of those who cannot live without the illusion of affairs or those so fearful of being ruled by others that they will pay away their lives to prevent it."[6] If it is necessary to secure their freedom, citizens of a liberal community will be self-governing. But if more freedom is to be found under a benevolent despot, who sees to public concerns and leaves our evenings free, the despot may be choice-worthy. It's just that despots are notoriously hard to control. Since we can't trust them, we must sometimes "pay away" our lives to check them; we must become active participants in public life—at least for a time. But that participation is never more than a necessary evil.

Finally, it is worth asking how prone to warlike activity such a society might be. In many ways the right answer seems to be that no community would be less warlike. Indeed, as Walzer writes, "the great advantage of liberal society may simply be this: that no one can be asked to die for public reasons or on behalf of the state."[7] Indeed, the traditional American dislike for conscription, for the idea that the political community can have a claim on our lives for a period of public service, is inherent in the liberal tradition (RP, 57). War is, then, a danger to liberal communities. In times of danger we have to band together, give up pursuit of private projects, and sacrifice for the common good. Those who are not enticed by the thought of common enterprises seem unlikely to be tempted by the ultimate common enterprise: war.

And yet critics of liberalism have noted that from the perspective of those seeking to govern a liberal society there may be temptation to think of war as something desirable. Governing a community of those who wish mainly to be left alone must often seem a thankless task, tempting one to seek ways of creating an artificial solidarity. What better way than a fit of patriotic sentiment brought on by the danger of an enemy? Indeed, if Berlin is correct to suggest that we have "a deep and incurable metaphysical need" to transform our private self with its individual vision and projects into a public self that sacrifices for others, we might suspect that a politically liberal society does violence to a profound ethical truth: We need cooperative endeavor to flourish as human beings. This element of human nature cannot perhaps be entirely suppressed, and the suppressed desire for solidarity may be suddenly and easily transformed—if the right occasion presents itself—into a desire to lose oneself in the cause of one's country. This will be especially true if "seepage" has corrupted the other bonds of association in which this basic human need might find some satisfaction.

An Ethical Politics: The Fraternal Community

The great alternative to the tradition of liberal individualism is the fraternal community, in which citizens take care to shape each other's character, in which the individual feels an emotional solidarity with the community, and in which it is possible to find one's "true self" by participating in the life of the larger community. In such a community statecraft will surely involve soulcraft. It is worth noting, though, that fraternal communities within Western history have often been paternal as well; it is, after all, government that must do the "crafting." Hence, it is not surprising that in explaining that statecraft must be soulcraft George Will should turn to the image of parents disciplining and shaping children. The tendency within some forms of Christian thought to take the commandment enjoining children to honor their parents as applicable also to political life is an example of the ease with which familial images may make their way into our conception of political community.

The ethical premise that underlies this vision of government—a true premise, I believe—is that the isolated individual is not fully human, and that there is a single good life in which one must participate in order to become fully human and overcome the deep division within the self. We should not overlook the kind of language—religious language—that seems appropriate here. Rousseau was one of the great theorists of fraternal community, and Walzer writes of Rousseau's social contract that it

> represents less an exchange than a moral transformation. . . . Into the state, according to this interpretation, a man brings the life which he has received from the bounty of nature and which is wholly his own. From the state, that is, from the shared experiences and general will of the political community, he receives a second life, a moral life, which is not his sole possession, but whose reality depends upon the continued existence of his fellow-citizens and of their association. (O, 91)

The citizen "belongs" to the fraternal community from which he has received his new and better self—a communal self now, no longer a self caught up in a world of private desires and projects. Walzer is correct, I think, to suggest that we *do* long for something like this and that liberal society fails to meet this important moral need of human nature. Berlin is equally correct, I think, to warn that such a common life, however we may long for it, can quickly become oppressive. Walzer writes: "Liberalism, even at its most permissive, is a hard politics because it offers so few emotional rewards; the liberal state is not a home for its citizens; it lacks warmth and intimacy" (RP, 68). True enough. But the implicit suggestion is that the political community should and might offer a "home"—might, that is, overcome the deep division within the self of which Berlin writes. And if our choices are between liberal individualism, which makes no such pretension, and fraternal solidarity's offer of a "home," those who have learned from Augustine's *City of God* ought to step to Berlin's side, though not without regret that so sensitive a companion as Walzer must disagree. We must say of the advocates of fraternal community what Augustine says of Sallust, whom he regarded as among the most honest of Roman historians: Even Sallust praised Rome too highly—which is not surprising, says Augustine, since he had no other city to praise (III,17).

If the tradition of political liberalism thinks of freedom as the way to virtue, the community of fraternal solidarity believes that virtue must be the way to freedom—or, at least, to "true freedom." It offers not the night-watchman state but the educative state. Virtue here is the first step, the primary commitment. Government—and citizens in their self-governing capacities— must take a concern to shape the virtue of the community's members. And if the liberal tradition had to hope that virtue would result from a commitment to freedom, it is just as true to say that the fraternal tradition can only hope that virtuous citizens will be jealous of each other's liberty, even the liberty of those less virtuous.

For this tradition it is virtue, not the virtues, that counts—civic virtue, a politicized concept of virtue. In Philip Abbott's words, citizens "throw themselves into the management of the republic and so, we are told, gain in the exhilaration of fraternity what they lose in their loss of self."[8] Indeed, when we think this way we may tend to equate virtue and civic virtue, the good citizen and the virtuous human being, ethics and politics. Such communities can be more successful in the inculcation of virtue, but only because they do not recognize that deep and incurable metaphysical tension that, for all its defects, the liberal tradition has seen: the tension between the individual made finally for God and the claims of any historical community.

It should be clear that within the tradition of fraternal solidarity participation in the public life of the community will be highly prized. Not because such participation is necessary if the community is to be healthy, nor because it is necessary to foster a common good, but simply because such participation *is* the common good. After all, in participating in the common life we set aside our self-interested individualism and find that better self who seeks his good only in the good of others. In losing our life within the community we find it—and find thereby in political activity a kind of salvation. We should be under no illusion that this can happen easily. Walzer suggests that the citizen characterized by civic virtue will be "the product of collective repression and self-discipline" (O, 232). But in that repression lies perfect freedom. This is the key to the educative state, the fraternal community: Only the virtuous are free, and the virtuous must first be shaped and disciplined. An important moral insight, true to the needs of our nature. But politically dangerous.

The necessary collective discipline may be most easily achieved and our sense of ourselves as participants in a collective undertaking most readily nourished when we perceive over against ourselves a common enemy. The intimacy of fraternal community, the sense of belonging it provides, requires the presence of outsiders. It is sobering to be reminded by Walzer of Hegel's insistence that the state achieves its true universality only in time of war and that war is therefore necessary for the ethical health of the political community (O, 184). Seeking in fraternal community a cure for the division *within* may require division *without,* outsiders over against whom our community can know itself as a community to which some belong because others do not.

Ethics and Politics: The Chalcedonian State

Liberal individualists are the Nestorians of our political tradition, tending to separate ethics and politics more than we ought. Proponents of fraternal solidarity are the Eutychians of our political tradition, seeking to blend politics and ethics more than we can and attempting a premature resolution of the tension between individual and community. What we need, then, is a Chalcedonian politics, which will neither separate nor confuse the ethical and the political.[9]

In its commitment to individual freedom the liberal tradition displays a sound political instinct, but in permitting that commitment to seep into and govern the whole of life it corrupts moral virtue. The tradition of fraternal community, reversing the error, makes human solidarity a goal to be reached by the political community. But there has been and can be a form of the liberal tradition that does not attempt to overcome the tension between ethics and politics, yet does recognize that there is indeed a tension. This form of the tradition claims that the public realm—the political—exists *not* just to support and make possible individual pursuit of private goals and projects, *nor* to foster fraternal solidarity. Rather, the political realm exists to foster *private, social* bonds—to make space in life for families, friendships, clubs, faiths, neighborhoods.

This vision does not think of individuals simply as bundles of interests. They are that, to some degree, of course, but they are also capable of forming social ties of great importance in human life, ties that can be corrupted or destroyed by too much autonomy. Nor does this vision contend that we can make no judgments about wherein the good life consists. But neither does this vision seek fraternal solidarity within political community. The goal of fraternity offers an ersatz closeness and depends on the notion that intimacy is secured by mutual devotion to one common goal. That sort of intimacy, however, easily becomes ideological and is easily combined with force.[10] By contrast, a genuine personal bond like friendship is unlikely to be focused on some single common goal and is almost certain to be destroyed by force. For this third vision there is no salvation to be gotten from the political—only the possibility of life within social bonds that, while not themselves salvation, may offer intimations of it. Freedom is not the way to virtue, nor virtue the road to freedom.

The concept of virtue that accompanies this understanding of individuals in community is not the civic virtue of fraternal solidarity; it is the older conception of the virtues as individual excellences that fit us for the many aspects of life in general. To think of virtues in this way—and to think such virtues important for human life—is already to commit ourselves to the view that political community should do more than foster private visions of autonomous individuals, for the development of virtuous habits of behavior will always require supporting social structures.[11] But there will be a diversity of virtues and a variety of life-styles that will rank and develop the virtues in different ways.

Consider, for example, the difference between fostering civic virtue in the form of fraternal solidarity and fostering the *private* bond of friendship. Friends need share no specific aims, are bound by no common goals, are ready and willing to receive the newcomer who shares their interests—they do not need the outsider to define themselves. They care about each other, not about the new and transformed self they receive from each other. By contrast, even when Walzer recognizes the importance of pluralism, he means by this primarily the importance of participation in other associations that have public aims and goals: labor unions, political parties, neighborhood associations. And if his pluralist citizen becomes politically unreliable because his loyalties are divided, this is primarily a matter of the citizen's personal honor and integrity, those cardinal modern virtues. Walzer's individuals are worried about their integrity and are seeking a new and better self in public life. But they are seldom simply loving and caring about others who are connected to them in private, non-goal-oriented ways. They are seldom individuals who may become politically dangerous not out of concern for their own integrity but simply because they love other people.

But people like these—the sort we seldom find in Walzer's depiction of fraternal community—are the citizens political community ought to foster. These will be citizens who know the meaning of sacrifice because they *have,* for example, sacrificed for their children. They will not simply be interested in making their own way in the world. To be sure, of course, they will not view political participation as a very great good except insofar as it sometimes nourishes their sense of sharing a common story—a common story, not a common goal—with still larger numbers of people. Nor are they likely to be very warlike unless those bonds that they value, bonds both social and private, are threatened. They are, that is, likely to be warlike primarily when on the defensive. They will fight for their homeland, not for their government. Knowing the family to be a quite different sort of community from the state, they are not likely to be persuaded that the fourth commandment has much to say about honoring political masters.

Dr. Johnson once said that "to be happy at home is the end of all human endeavor." That, I think, captures nicely this third vision of the relation of individual and community. To be happy at home—that is not a goal one can pursue autonomously or privately. But neither is it a political goal, though politics may be needed to make it possible. What it offers is genuine satisfaction of the human spirit, but still a partial satisfaction. For to be happy at home—in a genuine if small community bound together by love—is both to be happy and to be given an intimation of the real meaning of *home* for human beings, for home is that community in which all are loved personally by One who has the infinite resources to love all in that way. And we do not have to be possessive individualists to recognize that to try to find in any political community such a home is not just to fall prey to the "moral and political immaturity" of which Isaiah Berlin writes; it is, in the name of a noble moral ideal, to let loose in life a political demon. Better that we should seek to fashion a political order that will reckon with the several senses in which it is true that to be happy at home is the end of all human endeavor.

Notes

Chapter 2

1. C. S. Lewis, *The Voyage of the Dawn Treader* (New York: Macmillan, 1952). Page numbers for citations within these introductory paragraphs will be given in parentheses within the body of the text.

2. I have developed this theme in more detail in *The Taste for the Other: The Social and Ethical Thought of C. S. Lewis* (Grand Rapids: Eerdmans, 1978).

3. Stephen Crites, "The Narrative Quality of Experience," *Journal of the American Academy of Religion* 39 (1971): 291–311.

4. C. S. Lewis, "The Weight of Glory," in *The Weight of Glory and Other Addresses* (Grand Rapids: Eerdmans, 1965), pp. 12f.

5. C. S. Lewis, *Reflections upon the Psalms* (New York: Harcourt, Brace and World, 1958), p. 138. To fully develop Lewis's views we would have to note his belief that, apart from sin, our experience of the tension between our freedom and our finitude would not have been painful. Cf. Meilaender, *The Taste for the Other,* pp. 170–72.

6. C. S. Lewis, *Surprised by Joy* (New York: Harcourt, Brace and World, 1955), p. 218.

7. Cf. Chapter 5 of C. S. Lewis, *An Experiment in Criticism* (Cambridge: Cambridge University Press, 1969) and the essay "Myth Became Fact," in *God in the Dock,* ed. Walter Hooper (Grand Rapids: Eerdmans, 1970), pp. 63–67.

8. C. S. Lewis, "On Stories," in *Of Other Worlds,* ed. Walter Hooper (New York: Harcourt Brace Jovanovich, 1966), pp. 3–21.

9. Crites, "The Narrative Quality of Experience," pp. 301ff.

10. C. S. Lewis, "The Seeing Eye," in *Christian Reflections* (Grand Rapids: Eerdmans, 1967), p. 168.

11. C. S. Lewis, *Pilgrim's Regress* (Grand Rapids: Eerdmans, 1958).

12. The phrase is from the subtitle of Corbin Carnell's *Bright Shadow of Reality: C. S. Lewis and the Feeling Intellect* (Grand Rapids: Eerdmans, 1974).

13. Lewis, "On Stories," p. 15.

14. C. S. Lewis, "The Language of Religion," in *Christian Reflections*, p. 129.

15. Ibid., p. 130.

16. Lewis, "Myth Became Fact," p. 66.

Chapter 3

1. Martin Luther, "To the Christian Nobility of the German Nation Concerning the Reform of the Christian Estate," in *Luther's Works*, Volume 44 (Philadelphia: Fortress Press, 1966), pp. 201f.

2. Jack T. Sanders, *Ethics in the New Testament: Change and Development* (Philadelphia: Fortress Press, 1975), p. 8.

3. To think that we could overcome the tension would be to forget that theologians remain pilgrims. They may (and must) affirm the truth about reality revealed in Christ: that even the will of God that calls for our sanctification is a gracious will. They may (and must) affirm the truth of our experience within sinful history: that, while we can believe even the demanding God to be unequivocally gracious, we cannot fully experience him as such. The desire for absolute conceptual consistency within the whole theological task—the desire to surmount the tension between these two pictures—must therefore be labeled as gnostic. It is an attempt to leap beyond the boundaries of the Christian story and out of history before God brings that story to its close.

4. Paul Ramsey, *Basic Christian Ethics* (New York: Charles Scribner's Sons, 1950), p. 200.

Chapter 4

1. C. S. Lewis, *That Hideous Strength* (New York: Macmillan, 1946), p. 172.

2. Ibid., p. 174.

3. Reinhold Niebuhr, *The Nature and Destiny of Man,* Volume 1: *Human Nature* (New York: Charles Scribner's Sons, 1941), p. 17.

4. *The Confessions of St. Augustine,* trans. Rex Warner (New York: New American Library, 1963), XI, 28.

5. Crites, "The Narrative Quality of Experience," pp. 301ff.

6. Lewis Thomas, *The Medusa and the Snail* (New York: Viking Press, 1979), p. 63.

7. Ibid., p. 66.

8. Ibid., pp. 74ff.

9. Leon Kass, "Making Babies—The New Biology and the 'Old' Morality," *Public Interest* 26 (Winter 1972): 48f.

Chapter 5

1. Judith Jarvis Thomson, "A Defense of Abortion," *Philosophy and Public Affairs* 1 (Fall 1971): 47–66. Future references to this essay will be given by page number within parentheses in the body of the text.

2. The phrase is Iris Murdoch's in *The Sovereignty of Good* (London: Routledge and Kegan Paul, 1970), p. 48.

3. Annie Dillard, *Pilgrim at Tinker Creek* (New York: Harper's Magazine Press, 1974), p. 228.

4. Ibid., p. 229.

5. "Parasitology," in *The McGraw-Hill Encyclopedia of Science and Technology,* Volume 9 (New York: McGraw-Hill Books, 1971), p. 628.

6. "Parasitism," in *The Harper Encyclopedia of Science,* revised edition, ed. James R. Newman (New York: Harper and Row, 1967), p. 883.

7. Dillard, *Pilgrim at Tinker Creek,* p. 232.

8. Ibid., p. 176.

9. Gabriel Marcel, *Homo Viator* (New York: Harper Torchbooks, 1962), p. 87.

10. Augustine, *Concerning the City of God Against the Pagans,* trans. Henry Bettenson (New York: Penguin Books, 1972), XII, 3, 6.

11. "Parasitology," p. 628.

12. Thomas Hobbes, *Man and Citizen,* ed. Bernard Gert (Garden City, New York: Doubleday Anchor, 1972), VIII, 1. For similar imagery, cf. Lucretius, *De Rerum Natura,* V, 783–825.

13. *Romeo and Juliet,* II,ii,35–38,40,44.

Chapter 6

1. Catholic moral thought today is, of course, by no means mono-lithic. My discussion will for the most part assume a traditional Catholic position. But there has been considerable dissatisfaction with this view even within Catholic circles. In particular, many questions have been raised about the concept of indirect killing. For a readable account of varieties within current Catholic moral theology one might consult Chapter 5 of Charles Curran's *New Perspectives in Moral Theology* (Notre Dame: University of Notre Dame Press, 1976). Part of the discussion turns on the question of whether there may not be other values as basic as life. If there are, we would have to formulate a position that speaks of cases in which life conflicts with life *or* some value equivalent to life. This seems to me, however, an unpromising approach. However much difficulty we may have in formulating a hierarchy of rights or values, it would seem that life or a right to life—as a necessary prerequisite for the enjoyment of other values or the exercise of other rights—would be basic. Further-more, the new sorts of "conflict cases" created by equating other values with human life would fundamentally alter the Catholic position. For in these new conflict cases, unlike cases where life conflicts with equal life, killing would have to be direct. That is, the death of the fetus would have to be aimed at as part of one's plan. The other value, whatever it might be, would inevitably enter into consideration as a consequence to be attained by aiming at the fetus's death. As a result, any decision made in such new conflict cases would only be based (as Curran recognizes and makes clear) on a judgment of proportionate reason—that is, a weighing of costs and benefits involved. In terms of the categories used in this chapter, however, that would violate a negative duty for the sake of a positive duty.

2. Cf., for example, Ramsey's essay "The Morality of Abortion," in *Life or Death: Ethics and Options,* ed. Daniel H. Labby (Seattle: University of Washington Press, 1968). This essay was revised and reprinted in *Moral Problems,* ed. James Rachels (New York: Harper and Row, 1971).

3. There are a number of important problems that I do *not* take up here. I do not investigate the question of when an individual human life begins. My concern in this chapter is only to ask what circumstances would justify abortion after the point—whatever it may be—when we have among us another individual human life. Also, I do not take up certain difficult cases in any detail, e.g., cases of severe fetal deformation. A good discussion of that question is Paul F. Camenisch's "Abortion: For

the Fetus' Own Sake?" *Hastings Center Report* (April 1976): 38–41. Finally, I do not discuss the very important question about the way in which a moral position should or should not be reflected in codes of law.

4. Cf. Gerald Kelly, S.J., *Medico-Moral Problems* (St. Louis: Catholic Hospital Association of the U.S. and Canada, 1958), pp. 4ff.

5. Philippa Foot, "The Problem of Abortion and the Doctrine of Double Effect," in *Moral Problems,* ed. James Rachels (New York: Harper and Row, 1971), pp. 28–41.

6. Cf. Dale W. Cannon, "Ruminations on the Claim of Inenarrability," *Journal of the American Academy of Religion* 43 (1975): esp. 581.

7. C. S. Lewis, *The World's Last Night and Other Essays* (New York: Harcourt Brace Jovanovich, 1960), pp. 104f.

8. Paul Ramsey, "Abortion: A Review Article," *The Thomist* 37 (January 1973): 212.

9. Ibid., p. 214.

10. Helmut Thielicke, *The Ethics of Sex,* trans. John W. Doberstein (New York: Harper and Row, 1964), p. 239.

11. Paul Ramsey, *The Patient as Person* (New Haven: Yale University Press, 1970).

12. Ibid., p. 176.

13. Ibid., p. 187.

Chapter 7

1. Karl Barth, *Church Dogmatics,* Vol. III/4, ed. G. W. Bromiley and T. F. Torrance (Edinburgh: T. & T. Clark, 1961), p. 425.

2. I will be exploring some of the *moral* issues involved in euthanasia without taking up *legal* problems that also arise. I do not assume any answer to the question "Should what is morally wrong be legally prohibited?"

3. James Rachels, "Euthanasia," in *Matters of Life and Death: New Introductory Essays in Moral Philosophy,* ed. Tom Regan (New York: Random House, 1980), p. 29.

4. Nonvoluntary euthanasia occurs when the person euthanatized is in a condition that makes it impossible for him to express a wish (e.g., senile, comatose). Involuntary euthanasia occurs when the person euthanatized expresses a desire *not* to be killed but is nevertheless euthanatized.

5. Charles Fried, *Right and Wrong* (Cambridge: Harvard University Press, 1978), p. 27.

6. Cf. Joseph Butler, Dissertation "On the Nature of Virtue," appended to *The Analogy of Religion Natural and Revealed,* Morley's Universal Library edition (London: George Routledge and Sons, 1884), p. 301: "The fact then appears to be, that we are constituted so as to condemn falsehood, unprovoked violence, injustice, and to approve of benevolence to some preferably to others, abstracted from all consideration, which conduct is likely to produce an overbalance of happiness or misery; and therefore, were the Author of Nature to propose nothing to Himself as an end but the production of happiness, were His moral character merely that of benevolence; yet ours is not so." In other words, though the Creator may be a consequentialist, creatures are not! For a contrary view, see Peter Geach, *The Virtues* (Cambridge: Cambridge University Press, 1977), pp. 95ff.

7. Whether this enlargement of the scope of our responsibility really works is another matter. Being responsible for everything may, for human beings, come quite close to being responsible for nothing. Charles Fried comments: "If, as consequentialism holds, we were indeed equally morally responsible for an infinite radiation of concentric circles originating from the center point of some action, then while it might look as if we were enlarging the scope of human responsibility and thus the significance of personality, the enlargement would be greater than we could support. . . . Total undifferentiated responsibility is the correlative of the morally overwhelming, undifferentiated plasma of happiness or pleasure" (*Right and Wrong,* pp. 34f.).

8. It is a hard, perhaps unanswerable, question whether there might ever be exceptions to this general standard for Christian conduct. There might be a circumstance in which the pain of the sufferer was so terrible and unconquerable that one would want to consider an exception. To grant this possibility is not really to undermine the principle since, as Charles Fried has noted, the "catastrophic" is a distinct moral concept, identifying an extreme situation in which the usual rules of morality do not apply (*Right and Wrong,* p. 10). We would be quite mistaken to build the whole of our morality on the basis of the catastrophic; in fact, it would then become the norm rather than the exception. One possible way to deal with such extreme circumstances without simply lapsing into consequentialism is to reason in a way analogous to Michael Walzer's reasoning about the rules of war in *Just and Unjust Wars* (New York: Basic Books, 1977). Walzer maintains that the rules of war are binding even when they put us at a disadvantage, even when they may cost us victory. But he grants that there might be "supreme emergencies" in

which we would break the rules; namely, when doing so was (a) morally necessary (i.e., the opponent was so evil—a Hitler—that it was morally imperative to defeat him) and (b) strategically necessary (no way other than violating the rules of war was available for defeating this opponent). Reasoning in an analogous way we might wonder whether the rule prohibiting euthanasia could be transgressed if (a) the suffering was so severe that the sufferer lost all capacity to bear that suffering with any sense of moral purpose or faithfulness to God, and (b) the pain was truly unconquerable. Whether such extreme circumstances ever occur is a question I cannot answer. And even if such circumstances are possible, I remain uncertain about the force of this "thought experiment," which is offered tentatively.

9. This illustration is "inspired" by a different set of hypothetical cases offered by Paul Ramsey in "Some Rejoinders," *Journal of Religious Ethics* 4 (Fall 1976): 204.

10. The passages cited in this paragraph may be found scattered throughout pages 336–42 and 401–2 of Volume III/4 of Barth's *Church Dogmatics*.

11. For what follows, see C. S. Lewis, *Miracles* (New York: Macmillan, 1947), pp. 129ff., and Paul Ramsey, *The Patient as Person* (New Haven: Yale University Press, 1970), pp. 144ff.

12. Barth, *Church Dogmatics*, III/4, p. 368.

13. Ibid., p. 342.

14. George Orwell, "The Meaning of a Poem," in *My Country Right or Left, 1940–1943*, Volume 2 of *The Collected Essays, Journalism and Letters of George Orwell*, ed. Sonia Orwell and Ian Angus (New York: Harcourt Brace Jovanovich, 1968), p. 133.

15. For a strong statement of such a case, see James Rachels, "Active and Passive Euthanasia," *New England Journal of Medicine* 292 (1975): 78–80.

16. William May, "The Metaphysical Plight of the Family," in *Death Inside Out*, ed. Peter Steinfels and Robert M. Veatch (New York: Harper and Row, 1974), p. 51.

Chapter 8

1. Ramsey's position is spelled out in *Ethics at the Edges of Life* (New Haven: Yale University Press, 1978). McCormick's view is given fullest expression in two articles: "To Save or Let Die: The Dilemma of Modern

Medicine," *Journal of the American Medical Association* 229 (1974): 172–76; and "The Quality of Life, the Sanctity of Life," *Hastings Center Report* 8 (February 1978): 30–36. References to Ramsey's book and McCormick's article in the *Hastings Center Report* will be given by page number in parentheses within the body of the text.

2. Cf. Peter Winch, "The Universalizability of Moral Judgments," in *Ethics and Action* (London: Routledge and Kegan Paul, 1972), pp. 151–70. Nothing in my argument suggests that it would be morally permissible to *aim* at the death of oneself or another. I am discussing only treatment refusals that, though they might result in death, are intended as choices of other specifiable goods. Hence, I am *not* suggesting that the whole of morality is agent-relative and purely a matter for decision. Cf. Gilbert Meilaender, "Is What Is Right for Me Right for All Persons Similarly Situated?" *Journal of Religious Ethics* 8 (Spring 1980): 125–34.

3. John R. Connery, S.J., has pointed this out in his article "Prolonging Life: The Duty and Its Limits," *Linacre Quarterly* 47 (May 1980): 151–65. He asks, "Is it reasonable to make incompetent people bear burdens that competent people do not have to bear?" (p. 161). However, since Connery does not clearly recognize that decisions made by competent patients are just that—decisions, not discoveries—he falls back on "substituted judgment" in cases where decisions must be made for incompetents. Even here, however, he clearly accepts some of Ramsey's position, for he writes: "What must be kept in mind is that the proxy does not have the freedom the patient himself has regarding extraordinary means" (p. 157).

Chapter 9

1. The President's Commission for the Study of Ethical Problems in Medicine and Biomedical and Behavioral Research, *Deciding to Forego Life-Sustaining Treatment* (Washington, D.C.: Government Printing Office, 1982), p. 190.

2. Sidney H. Wanzer, M.D., et al., "The Physician's Responsibility Toward Hopelessly Ill Patients," *New England Journal of Medicine* 310 (April 12, 1984): 958.

3. See a discussion of the first two cases in Bonnie Steinbock, "The Removal of Mr. Herbert's Feeding Tube," *Hastings Center Report* 13 (October 1983): 13–16; also see George J. Annas, "The Case of Mary Hier: When Substituted Judgment Becomes Sleight of Hand," *Hastings Center Report* 14 (August 1984): 23–25.

4. Daniel Callahan, "On Feeding the Dying," *Hastings Center Report* 13 (October 1983): 22.

5. Joanne Lynn and James Childress, "Must Patients Always Be Given Food and Water?" *Hastings Center Report* 13 (October 1983): 18.

6. Michael Walzer, *Just and Unjust Wars* (New York: Basic Books, 1977), p. 146.

Chapter 10

1. James Nelson, *Embodiment: An Approach to Sexuality and Christian Theology* (Minneapolis: Augsburg Publishing House, 1978). References to this book will be given by page number within parentheses in the body of the text.

2. C. S. Lewis, *The Screwtape Letters, with Screwtape Proposes a Toast* (New York: Macmillan, 1961), p. 101.

3. Lisa Sowle Cahill, *Between the Sexes: Foundations for a Christian Ethics of Sexuality* (Philadelphia: Fortress Press, and New York: Paulist Press, 1985), p. 92.

4. Ibid., p. 97.

5. Ibid.

6. John Updike, *Too Far to Go: The Maples Stories* (New York: Fawcett Crest, 1979), p. 10.

7. Ibid., p. 179.

Chapter 11

1. George F. Will, *Statecraft as Soulcraft: What Government Does* (New York: Simon and Schuster, 1983).

2. Isaiah Berlin, *Four Essays on Liberty* (London: Oxford University Press, 1969), p. 172. Hereafter abbreviated as FEL.

3. My scheme is considerably influenced by Philip Abbott's *Furious Fancies: American Political Thought in the Post-Liberal Era* (Westport, Connecticut: Greenwood Press, 1980).

4. Michael Walzer, *Radical Principles: Reflections of an Unreconstructed Democrat* (New York: Basic Books, 1980), p. 69. Hereafter abbreviated as RP.

5. The language describing selves as "bundles of interests" or "repositories of imaginative possibilities" is taken from Abbott, *Furious Fancies,* p. 243.

6. Michael Oakeshott, "Introduction" to Hobbes's *Leviathan* (Oxford: Basil Blackwell, 1955), p. lxiv.

7. Michael Walzer, *Obligations: Essays on Disobedience, War, and Citizenship* (New York: Simon and Schuster, 1970), p. 89. Hereafter abbreviated as O.

8. Abbott, *Furious Fancies,* p. 40.

9. Nestorius, patriarch of Constantinople in the fifth century, was thought to hold a view that separated the two natures in Christ so sharply as to question the oneness of the person. Eutyches, archimandrate of a cloister in Constantinople, held that after the incarnation Christ had only one nature. The formulation settled on at the Council of Chalcedon in 451 rejected both these views.

10. Abbott, *Furious Fancies,* p. 245.

11. Ibid., p. 40.

Index